SUSIE SEXPERT'S
LESBIAN SEX WORLD

SUSIE SEXPERT'S LESBIAN SEX WORLD

Susie Bright

CLEIS
PRESS
PITTSBURGH•SAN FRANCISCO

Published in the United States by Cleis Press Inc., P.O. Box 8933, Pittsburgh, Pennsylvania 15221, and P.O. Box 14684, San Francisco, California 94114.

Printed in the United States.
Cover and text design: Ellen Toomey
Cover photo: Jill Posener, Courtesy of Stormy Leather
Typesetting: CaliCo Graphics
Logo art: Juana Alicia

10 9 8 7 6
ISBN: 0-939416-34-4 cloth
ISBN: 0-939416-35-2 paper

Grateful acknowledgment is made to *On Our Backs* and *Lambda Rising Book Report* for permission to reprint essays which originally appeared in those magazines.

ACKNOWLEDGMENTS

I 'd like to thank the following friends for teaching me a thing or two about sex:

My partners in *On Our Backs*, Debi Sundahl and Nan Kinney; Joani Blank and her Good Vibrations phenomenon; Joelle Vidal, Eric Hodderson, Willie Grover, Honey Lee Cottrell, and Carter Herrera.

Special thanks to sister Lisa LaBia for her assistance and support in preparing this anthology.

ABOUT THE AUTHOR

S usie Bright—dubbed the Pauline Kael of porn—is one of the best known erotic critics and lesbian sex educators in America. She is the editor of *On Our Backs*, the magazine for the "adventurous" lesbian, and the editor of *Herotica* (Down There Press), an anthology of erotica. Her columns appear in *On Our Backs*, and her X-rated movie reviews appeared in *Penthouse Forum* from 1986 to 1989.

CONTENTS

MEET SUSIE SEXPERT:

AN INTRODUCTION

S usie Sexpert was born out of a temper tantrum, and a righteous festering one at that. I wrote my first "Toys for Us" column chronicling the world of lesbian sex for the debut issue of *On Our Backs* in 1984, the first magazine for the "adventurous" lesbian. I was hopping mad over the biggest lie ever told since the world was proclaimed flat: lesbians don't have sex.

Oh, lesbians have been accused of being sensual, even erotic; the way you might describe a pretty soap bubble. But the substance of sex—the sweat-pouring-off-you, the "She's Gotta Have It" variety—that's something the daughters of Sappho have had a hard time showing off.

Now some of the fault for this lie belongs to dumb straight people. When I tell them I edit a lesbian sex magazine, their favorite response is, "Lesbian sex? Isn't that a contradiction in terms?" My partner, Debi, calls these people "The Three-Minute Fucks," and they've got a three-minute consciousness to go along with it.

But the rest of the blame belongs to dumb dykes. And you know who you are. . . Or, who you were, because at some time nearly all of us have been dumb dykes. "Speak for yourself," you say—and so I will. I received a typical little girl education about sex, and it went something like this:

1) Girls don't know very much about sex, and they don't need to know more.

2) Girls need love, not sex.

3) Don't expect to come.

The early women's liberation movement threw these notions in the trash, and sooner than you could say "eat my clit," women were revealing their sexual appetites in unprecedented numbers. From the "myth of the vaginal orgasm," most clearly demolished in Shere Hite's first *Report*, to the lesbian sex manifestoes, such as "In Amerika They Call Us Dykes," in *Our Bodies, Ourselves*, uppity women made their sexual truths known. Betty Dodson, a New York artist, made herstory with her first illustrated pamphlet, *Liberating Masturbation*, in which she challenged readers to call up their mothers to demand, "Mom, are you masturbating to orgasm?"

In a vulva-shaped nutshell, the message was find your clit, learn to create your orgasm, express your sexual curiosity to its fullest, and don't let anyone, especially any man, tell you how or when to get off. So there! A militant, hands-on start to women's sexual liberation.

But lies and fears die hard. While the new generation of feminist lesbians were eager to talk about themselves— and equally eager to set a new standard for female sexual identity—we came up a little shy and little short describing what lesbians actually do in bed. Instead, there was the big distraction: "What We Don't Do," i.e., heterosexuality. And what defined heterosexuality? Masculinity? What's that exactly? Oh, what a nasty trap we fell into.

Lesbian-feminist sex theory reduced itself to purging anything aggressive, vicarious, and non-oval-shaped from its erotic vocabulary. The mainstream lesbian media mouthed sexist clichés about the "nature of men and women" that could have come out of a fundamentalist pulpit. And as the schism in feminist sexual politics grew wider in the eighties, that is exactly what happened.

Men were typically described as inherently aggressive, naturally promiscuous and objectifying, exclusively genitally focused; prone to sexual addictions, dangerous pornographic masturbation, and in general, needing to be contained so that their active pursuit of sexuality wouldn't be a public menace.

Women, on the other hand, were lauded for our inherently sexual gentility and monogamous nature, equating our desire with romantic love, our sex with a nurturing, non-genitally focused sensuality. Sexual pleasure and liberation were absolutely not priorities for women. Finally, women never used, produced or enjoyed pornography.

And if you believe any of the above, I've got a great little piece of property to show you on Love Canal. . .

These theoretical premises created the opportunity for traditional right-wingers to use conservative feminist rhetoric to seduce liberals and naive bystanders into fighting the "evil" of pornography. Liberal America might be willing to let go of the notion that "women's place is in the home," but the idea that women needed to be defended from "pornographic violence"—the new euphemism for "the evil in men's hearts"—was a media winner.

No less a feminist than Ed Meese, Ronald Reagan's right hand morals man, found the women's anti-porn movement so attractive that he invited its leader, Andrea Dworkin, to testify at a series of hearings designed to void the First

Amendment in regard to sexual expression, and roll back the last twenty years of progress in sexual discussion and sexual civil rights. The Meese Commission Report, two fat volumes of testimony, contain a surreal mixture of religious fundamentalist and vice squad feminist babbling—interspersed with some of the wildest, wettest smut they could dig up. I myself came three times by the end of the first volume, but my few moments of genitally focused, single minded pleasure were grossly interrupted by the non-stop marriage proceedings between the worst of right-wing and liberal protectionist rhetoric.

Meanwhile, in the private lives of women, sexual discoveries were making their own tracks, erotic power was blooming—but hardly anybody talked about it. Good Vibrations, the unique women's vibrator store where I worked for five years, was an explosive confessional. Every day, in the guise of selling vibrators, dildos, erotic books, and lubricants, I talked to women in detail about their sexual lives. Women revealed outrageous ignorance and self-doubt (even self-censure)—but these were the folks who took a chance to even come into such a place.

As it turned out, the number one sexual concern of most women is that they don't orgasm, or that they can't control when or how they do. Men do not lament that they don't know how to orgasm, or if they have ever gotten off. Never. That's not biology; that's oppression.

In my conversations with women at Good Vibes, a little knowledge went a long way. It was almost embarrassing to simply show a woman a diagram of her G-spot and clitoris, and watch twenty years of anxiety slip away.

Lesbian relationships unleashed all the passion and problems of women's sexual experience to the "nth" degree. Even lesbians who weren't indoctrinated by feminism too often had their sexual lives ruled by secrecy and shame.

You don't have to have a position paper in your hand to explain why you might be embarrassed and fearful of your sexual desires. Women are infected with sexual self doubt from childhood on, and a predisposition to lesbianism is no ticket out of traditional feminine mistrust and ignorance of sexual priorities. The feminist dykes couldn't look their desires in the face either—what was the "right" way to have sex? The "right way" looked to be as expansive as the head of a pin. The first time I told a lip-biting lesbian couple over the dildo counter that "penetration is only as heterosexual as kissing," I saw a flash flood.

Another group of women appeared at the same time in the early eighties, a surprisingly diverse bunch of women who plugged in their Magic Wands singing, "The Truth Will Set You Free." Their spirit embodied the sexual revolution I'd been yearning for, and all that Susie Sexpert has expressed. These women—some of my generation, some older—realized we hadn't instigated a revolution to just sit back and say, "No sex please, we're lesbians." We had the zeal of our political missionary and social work backgrounds. Other women—and these gals fascinated me—completely ignored the agonizing stages I had gone through and simply accepted the benefits of gay and women's liberation, asking only one question: "What else?" They demanded the products, services and social life befitting sexually liberated and self-accepting human beings. They rejected the notion that they should suffer any longer for gratification. Some elders found them ungrateful and apolitical, but I found them refreshing, the evidence that we did indeed change the world.

The satisfaction of introducing women to the words that describe our sexual lives, to the pictures of our bodies and desires, to the confidence of hearing other women's common and kinky sexual experiences—well, there's been no turning back. Sexually, there is nothing new under the sun. But there are still so many shadows, and it has been the talking and writing and revealing that have cast us into the light.

A little on the history of Susie Sexpert's column in *On Our Backs:* Nearly all of these collected essays appeared as a column called "Toys for Us." " Toys for Us " started out as a one shot deal for the birth of a lesbian erotic magazine. I dabbled at playing Dear Abby, but soon grew too impatient to wait for yesterday's postmarked questions. Sometimes I reveled in compiling a Lesbian Consumer Reports of sex toys, but as time I went on, I was more interested in the ins and outs of intimate lesbian life than I was in erotic popular mechanics.

"Toys for Us" has lived though the bloom in women's erotica, lesbian videos and lesbian "porn stars," feminist S/M, the revelation of the G-spot, the New Butch/Femme and the even-newer Lipstick Lesbians, the Meese Commission sex wars, AIDS and safer sex—and now five years later, I've got pregnancy and motherhood to push my pen around. Will Susie Sexpert's World of Lesbian Sex turn into the New Donna Reed Show? Get a fresh diaper and wipe that smile off your face.

Susie Bright
February 1990

THE FIRST TIME

SUMMER 1984

Gallup Polls have never found it fit to ask what sex toys are most popular among lesbians. Neither has *Consumer Reports*. However, with the debut of *On Our Backs*, fascinating statistics and well-informed exaggerations will now be available at every dyke's fingertips.

For some lucky girls, improvised sex toys were an integral part of childhood sexuality. Doctor's exams were only the tip of the iceberg. Remember little Felice, who happily saddled her mother's vibrating washing machine every time a full load was put in? Or how about Michele, who stuffed a patent leather high-heeled shoe into her drawers and traipsed around the house until she was delirious? For children of the sixties like myself, stories of electric toothbrushes were common to the point of mundane.

Yet even with these promising introductions to the world of sexual aids, most young women abandoned what they thought were babyish dolls and dildos as they approached puberty; or worse yet, abandoned masturbation altogether.

For those who sealed their Pandora's playbox, or who never opened it to begin with, now is the time to redeem yourselves. Yes, I know the protest that's on the tip of your tired lips, "But, I don't *need* a vibrator!"

Of course you don't. You don't *need* to have fun. You don't *need* to have incredible sensations and adventures. A little water and seventeen-grain bread will probably get you along in life just fine. Rather than be concerned with the survivalist in one's life, I propose to concern ourselves with our wants, dreams, impulses, and most particularly, *desires*. A vibrator is an entrée to a desirable experience. So is a dildo. So is a skimpy little outfit, a marabou feather, fragrant warm oils, and a butt plug on the side. With a little bit of consumer information and a healthy craving to please herself, every lesbian now has the opportunity to explore the world of sexual playthings.

Let's talk about basic household appliances. Plug-in vibrators are clearly favored over battery models for the following reasons:

a) they last for years;

b) they give a strong, smooth, consistent vibration; and

c) they are made by well-known companies that are accountable to their customers.

Battery-operated vibrators offer certain styles and sensations that can be a lot of fun, but you will never forgive the little sucker when it conks out at the crucial moment. In general, battery models last months, not years, and their power is much weaker than the electric vibrators. Of course, there are a few noteworthy exceptions, but the point is, open the treasure chest and *try* something.

A dildo can be a succulent squash, or a tender mold of silicon. Technically, it is any device you use for the pleasure of vaginal or anal penetration. It should be made of an easy-to-clean non-irritating material, and hopefully something that will warm to your skin as you use it. I once had a terrible ordeal with a carrot right out of the refrigerator.

Once you settle down with your preferred model, you will find that while lacking the dexterity of your fingers, dildos are tireless little helpers that can greatly enhance the variety of penetration you enjoy and might even add a whole new caseload to your fantasy file.

The facts about dildos aren't nearly as controversial as their famous resemblance to the infamous "penis" and all that *it* represents. The political, social, and emotional connotations of dildos have many unhappy lesbians in a stranglehold. I once received an anguished letter from a dyke couple in Palo Alto who said that their sex life was satisfying except for one tiny matter.

"We seem to be suffering with some hangover from our heterosexual past that makes us both want sensation in our vaginas apart from direct clitoral stimulation. As much as I try to put it out of my mind, this keeps coming up between us. Could you please send us some *very* discreet information about dildos?"

Ladies, the discreet, complete and definitive information on dildos is this: penetration is only as heterosexual as kissing. Now that truth can be known! Fucking knows no gender.

Not only that, but penises can only be compared to dildos in the sense that they take up space. Aside from difference in shape and feel, the most glaring contrast is that the dildo is at your service; it knows no desire other than your own or your partner's. Too many lesbians try on the dildo and harness in the Good Vibrations' dressing room and expect the device to take off with a life of its own. That might be exciting for a couple of sessions, but truthfully, it is more satisfying to take the time, trial and pleasant error to find out how to maneuver your own dildo for optimal pleasure.

Soon you'll find yourself with a whole collection of rubber dollies, and will be reduced to giving them pet names: "Where is Henri?" "Has Boom-Boom been cleaned yet?" And, "How could you lend out Amelia?"

G-SPOT JITTERS

FALL 1984

Dear Susie Sexpert:
I can't find my G-spot and I've looked everywhere.
I wouldn't even believe the stupid thing existed except
that my girlfriend gets off on hers every time we make
love. She loves to get fucked hard in this special area,
and then when she orgasms, she squirts out come like
a fire hydrant. It looks like so much fun. Why can't
I find mine?

Miserable in Miami

Dear Missy:
Your girlfriend must have been one of the women
the research team mentioned in Dr. Beverly Whipple's
book, *The G-Spot*, the little paperback that's caused such
a fuss. Halfway through the text, Dr. Whipple thanks a
special group of Miami lesbians for sharing their G-spot
experiences with the curious doctors.

While *The G-Spot* was reassuring and enlightening for

women who orgasm through vaginal penetration, it left other women skeptical and worried as to where this magic elevator button is and how it works.

The more complete picture is that the spot is actually a sponge, a bean-sized item that fills with blood during sexual arousal. It also surrounds and protects the urethra from undue pressure. This spot is a couple of inches above your pubic bone and directly in front of your uterus. An outstanding diagram of the whole business can be found in *A New View of a Woman's Body*, illustrated by Suzann Gage, the best self-help handbook to come out since *Our Bodies, Ourselves*.

A New View of a Woman's Body takes a more comprehensive view of the G-spot, naming it the urethral sponge and defining it as part of the clitoris. This means that the clitoris is not just a little nubby kernel peeking out of a hood, but rather an entire system of sexually responsive parts which extend internally along the vaginal wall surrounding the urethra and parts of the bladder: erectile tissue, muscle, nerves, and blood vessels.

Consequently, while every woman's clitoris is sensitive to sexual arousal, each woman is different in terms of how she likes to be tickled. Some women like stimulation to the heads of their clits, some want an intensive G-spot rubdown, and others want the flat side of a tongue on the left side of their labia! Our cunts are strong individualists. Sure, you have a G-spot, but that may not be your cup of tea.

Still, you say, you feel like you're missing out on all the fun. The old sex motto, "Practice Makes Orgasm," once again applies.

When you're alone, try using an vibrator or dildo to reach your G-spot. Remember, it's not very far up, but it's tricky to reach with your own fingers unless you have very long digits and a short vagina. If you're with a partner, have her insert fingers while you lie on your belly.

Press, rub, and pitter-patter the spongy portion of your anterior vaginal wall. Feel like you have to go to the bathroom? Perfect! Keep pushing on that sensation, feel the sponge grow harder and larger and imagine you are going to flood the room with your orgasm. A lot of women get hung up at this stage because of their reluctance to wet the bed, make a mess, or embarrass the relatives. Too bad! It's now or never to have your very own, self-righteous, it's-about-time, G-spot orgasm.

Some women will come this way without ejaculating anything. Others will say that they're too busy being happily clit-tickled or ass-fucked to be bothered with any G-spot gyrations. Women who do come with an ejaculation should be reassured that this fluid is not urine, but rather a substance similar to semen without sperm.

The whole scholarly intention of the G-spot book was to prove that women and men are more sexually similar in their biology than our culture implies, and I agree with them. The G-spot/urethral sponge is analogous to the male prostate gland, which is an orgasmic area for men reached through the anus instead of the cock.

Isn't sex fascinating? I hope Ms. in Miami finds her sexual niche, wherever it may be.

VIBRATOR ADDICT

WINTER 1985

Dear Susie Sexpert:
I'm worried that if I start using a vibrator I'm not going to be able to quit and come naturally again. I know one lady who can only have an orgasm with her Magic Wand, and I don't want to end up like her.

Restless Rita

Dear Rusty,
      Unlike free-basing or biting your nails, using a vibrator is neither physiologically addictive nor a nervous habit. We live in an addiction-prone culture and it often seems something is hardly worth doing if you can't get hooked on it. But I think you will find vibrators to be a liberating experience after all.

Most human beings tend to adopt a sexual pattern of expression which they cling to like a leaf once they find that it reliably gives them orgasms. For example, yours truly masturbated from ages eight to eighteen in the exact same position: belly down, hand crammed under a perfectly rigid body, with one social finger moving over the head of my clit. This wasn't such a bad position for a child, but as I grew bigger this practice nearly broke my arm and caused me much grief. I didn't know how else to have an orgasm and my futile tries at other methods were a bust.

My first vibrator experience, on the other hand, was a tremendous awakening. I could enjoy its intensity in all kinds of ways I had never felt before. Vibrators *broke* my "sex pattern" and once I made this first change, all sorts of subtle and more outrageous variations opened up to me. You will find plenty of women with the same story.

Yes, vibrators will often let you orgasm faster than other methods. Ultimately, though, a hot fantasy in the hand will still beat an apathetic vibrator in the bush. Just imagine combining the best of both worlds!

Women who feel they are getting stuck in a rut with their vibrators, or any other sex practice they may believe has become a bad habit, can try the stop-and-start method. Begin by using your vibrator as usual, but when you feel close to your brink, turn it off and continue with your hand or your partner. Keep going back and forth between the different methods, letting your arousal play from one stimulation to another. By this time you will find that it can be both extremely pleasurable and maddening to delay your orgasm through the stop-and-start exercise.

Another suggestion, should you want to set aside your vibrator, is to pick out something sexy to read or look at while you play with yourself. I just brought home an album called "Talk Dirty To Me" by porn star Sharon Mitchell, which seems perfect for experimenting with aural sex.

Listen, there are vibrator lovers out there who never came at all before they bought their toys. You'd have a lot of nerve to condemn their satisfaction as being unnatural or addictive. Sexual repression and lack of sensual feeling are what's epidemic and sick in our little world. It is both a Susie Sexpert and scientific fact that more orgasms lead to *more orgasms*, and here lies the greatest virtue of buzzing off.

PACK IT UP, I'LL TAKE IT

SPRING 1985

Dear Susie Sexpert:
Until recently I considered myself just another butch dyke. I'm into 501 jeans, leather, moderate S/M, and pretty women. However, I've found a new fetish that is very unsettling. While at home one day, curiosity prompted me to put my dildo in my 501's and wear it around the house. The contrived bulge was a major turn-on. I liked the way I looked and I liked the way I felt. Rubbing my hand over my prominent crotch, I had an explosive orgasm.
My strong reaction to this experience raised a few questions. How do I incorporate this desire into my feminist ideology? As a feminist with a degree in psychology, it was my belief that Freud lost all credence after his discourse on penis envy. (Maybe I should re-evaluate my criticism of Dr. Freud's theory.) Am I alone or do other lesbians have similar fantasies? Would I be the object of severe ridicule if I were to wear my fantasy out in public? Please tell

me all you can about this subject.

Jumpin' Jacki

Dear J.J.:

What a hot little treat your letter was! I think many fretful butches have had feelings similar to yours.

The real question is: How can feminist ideology incorporate *your* desires? As helpful as feminism has been in explaining gender differences, it has not yet developed as a philosophy that explains sexuality, or the erotic.

Understanding why you are making fifty-nine cents to every man's dollar is hardly the jumping-off point to determining the source of your lust. What women's liberation has given to us sexually is the idea that we should be in control of our own bodies, and that we are capable and credible in determining our sexual preferences.

I don't think you have penis envy, I think you have dildo envy. How many times do I have to repeat the basics? A dildo is *not* a penis. Look at both items sometime and you'll immediately notice the differences. For starters, a dildo is a sexual plaything; it is not attached to a human body who has to live with it till death. Keep in mind that it was rubbing your play-cock against your *clitoris* that got you off.

Do you realize that dildos are among the few pieces of sexual turf historically associated with dykes? Everyone uses them but it's us lezzies who made them famous. It's your goddess-given right to use dildos; it's your damn heritage, in fact.

Will you be ridiculed if you pack a dildo in public? Well, you might be the source of more dildo envy. But I think your pleasure might be worth it. In fact, there's this lovely little restaurant I know, where we could meet and. . .

Lovingly,
Susie Sexpert

Dear Susie Sexpert:

Please explain the physio/sexual/social dynamics when "butch meets butch." I have seen extremely repelling reactions and I've also witnessed very positive results. What are your comments?

New Jersey

Dear Jersey:

My friend Fanny Fatale, outspoken lesbian stripper and self-defined butch/femme expert, begged me to let her answer this important question.

Fanny says: "When butch meets butch and it's positive, their masculine psyches say, 'You're like me. That turns me on (sexual). Let's get it on (social).'"

Sometimes butch meets butch, and they will look the other way for a femme. I learned the hard way that you cannot judge a butch by her cover. They are not all attracted to femmes. Even if they are, they are not all (indeed few are) aggressive in the sack. That can be confusing and complicated at first, but realizing that butch/butch or femme/femme is just as common as butch/femme makes for happier relationships in the long run.

What would one butch say to another if they were talking dirty? "I'll suck your dick if you suck mine." Or, "I know that underneath you're just a cunt who wants to be laid down and fucked, so bend over."

Here's another thought to make your brain tilt: There are butches who dress in feminine clothes because it turns them on. Who is really in drag? A butch in masculine clothes or a butch wearing feminine clothes? What will determine drag in our enlightened sexual future?

Here's another: Half of the lesbians who work in the sex industry as erotic dancers or prostitutes are butches. Butches in feminine disguise. To the trained femme eye, this is as obvious as nakedness.

31

ASS FORWARD

SUMMER 1985

I'd like to address the subject of anal sex. It used to be that any time a customer squirmed around in the vibrator store without saying a word, I could be sure that it had to do with her ass.

Nowadays, there has literally been a popular revolution in openness about anal sex. People will candidly admit to the bumper sticker philosophy, "I'd Rather Be Butt Fucking." Well, some people.

Most of all, everyone has questions: Does it have to hurt? What if I break something? Is it true that people have to go to the emergency room to get various objects removed?

Why don't lesbians talk much about anal sex? We know it isn't "ladylike," and it brings up larger-than-usual fears about cleanliness and disease. No one, gay or straight, is given any information about anal sexuality, even though it can be as orgasmic and fulfilling as any other kind of sex.

I have seen some excellent anal sex articles in lesbian sex rags other than *On Our Backs*, but they are all geared towards elbow-length fisting, rather than the more common concerns of Jane Doe, who is simply trying to apply her pinkie to The Last Frontier.

It's really quite simple. The main idea is that your ass actively receives and opens up to penetration through relaxation and arousal. It cannot be pushed open like a vagina, which, let's be frank, can more easily be shoved around. No, your anus must definitely make the first move.

Anal foreplay, sometimes the best part, is playing with the crack between the cheeks and the sensitive little wrinkles that surround the hole. This is the perfect time to start dabbling in vegetable oil. You want oodles of lubricant, so be generous. Your rectum and anus do not provide wetness aside from the sweat of anticipation. You can't use too much lube.

Moving into the asshole is where you definitely need to speak up. (Masturbators can conveniently skip this step.) The old anal sex motto, "lubrication and communication," should be your guide. Check in with your partner to see how it's feeling and where to go from here.

Let's say you want your lover to stick her index finger just a little way in, and then hold it there, absolutely motionless for a couple of minutes until your anus is completely relaxed. Then perhaps you want her to change tactics and thrust into you with hard, downward strokes. Maybe you want her to move another finger inside very slowly just before you come. With all these variations and preferences, you can see that there is no way to get around talking. No lover is able to look into your eyes and figure out how you want to get fucked in the ass.

The exquisite feelings you may have with anal penetration have to do with the fullness in your ass and the pressure on your perineal sponge, the underbelly of your clitoris. Your whole clit may very well be rock hard, especially if you've got hands in other places.

Fingers or objects that are inserted into the rectum should be utterly smooth and free of abrasion. It doesn't matter how big it is; what matters is whether it's scratchy. A little tear inside your anus or rectum could be infected by the feces that pass through. Next time you see a well-manicured pair of hands, you'll know where they've been.

If you use a dildo, make sure it has a flared base, which acts as a stopper to prevent it from slipping all the way into your rectum.

This is the way people lose things up their butts: A woman comes into the vibrator store and buys a tiny, slim vibrator with no base on its end. She thinks it will be an enormous task to slip even the head of the toy into her ass. Surprise, surprise, she finds herself so relaxed and ecstatic that she accidentally slips the entire vibrator into her rectum and doesn't notice until after she's come. Now, she could just bear down and push it out, but the outrageousness of the episode might very well cause her to panic.

Next stop, hospital room; with a red face and a tight ass. The doctor will dilate her rectum and retrieve the toy. End of story, and I hope my message is clear. Use your hands or a dildo with a flared base and you will never have to make an exotic hospital visit.

Some lovers like to use diamond-shaped butt plugs which have the advantage of being easily "worn" while their hands are free for other tasks. But if your favorite part is the thrusting action, then you can use whatever shape dildo pleases you. Any adult sex shop will carry these, by the way. As I say, they are all the rage.

Between you and me, more and more heterosexuals are coming in with the husband wanting to get fucked in the ass and the wife happy to oblige. What startling progress!

A few words about cleanliness. . . if you don't know by now not to stick your buttplug or finger into your cunt until it's clean, you'd better go back to *Our Bodies, Our-selves*. If the idea of getting a few specks of shit on your paw unnerves you, it's time to grow up. More serious anal enthusiasts will do a small douche or enema to cleanse any fecal debris, but this isn't necessary for your average en-counter—average being, say, up to three fingers wide and four to six inches long. Of course, if you're feeling raw or extra tender, come in out of the rain. Use your head and you will avoid the many pitfalls of anal mystiques and myths.

BOSS CITY

FALL 1985

I arrived in Chicago in July of 1985 to be greeted by a crackling hailstorm. Within an hour the city had been relieved of a miserable heat wave and I enjoyed a week of near perfect weather. And in perfect weather, Chicago is one the most beautiful cities in the world.

I'll never understand why my ex-Chicagoan friend Rhonda warned us before leaving, "If you want to be around gay people, why are you going to Chicago?" Nonsense. The gay community in the Windy City is unique and has a long history.

The biggest surprise to me is that Chicago has more lesbian bars than any other major city in the country. Your standard disco cruise-out, best exemplified by Augie and C.K.'s, is just another drop in the bucket, along with the softball players' bars, the "wrinkle" bars, the wall-to-wall drinking bars, airport suburban bars, and the we'll-try-anything-once places like His 'N Hers, which hosted our lesbian sex videos during my stay, but has also showcased everything from folk music to Pudding Wrestling matches.

37

People complain about the limitations of bar social life, but for a newcomer like me, the whole town seemed bursting with ready-made places to meet women of every description. There's also a sizable counterculture of gay men and women mixing together; refreshing after the strict segregationist attitudes of San Francisco and New York.

In general, Chicago reflects the best and worst of gay life as it was ten years ago in gay meccas like San Francisco. Butches and femmes casually carry out their relationships and erotic styles. If the younger feminist crowd has anything to say about it, you don't hear them because they are extremely isolated. You either have your Women's Studies diploma or you don't give a shit.

The same old-style gay life that is so accepting of butch/femme is extremely closeting for the S/M community. The night we showed the sex videos at His 'N Hers, friends came up to me, whispering, "There are now eight S/M women here"—but how could you tell? No leather, not a pinch of it. If you're an S/M dyke, you keep your lip buttoned about it, and live through your fantasies until maybe one day you'll meet another lone woman who feels the same as you. People won't even wear contemporary leather as fashion for fear that their reputations will be ruined.

The big exception is the suburban women. . . What a mystique they have! Apparently these wild suburb lezzies have fuckerware parties, freely dressing up in lingerie and studs. Even the butches wear dresses. Since I stayed strictly in the gay ghetto for my entire visit, I'm afraid I can't report a first-hand experience, but the rumors were titillating.

Chicago women were forthright. They'd tell me their opinions to my face, and I didn't dare take them personally. If they didn't like the sex flicks, then they loved my legs. If they loved *On Our Backs*, they told me exactly what stories and models were their favorites.

Another must-see on your Chicago tour is the Baton Show Lounge, notorious as offering the best drag show in the country. The performers are simply outstanding and the audience is an eye-opener all to themselves.

The Baton offers a thoroughly professional cabaret, with the type of female impersonation that makes you realize what an utterly sexual novelty gender is. When performer Chili Pepper, a crowd favorite, sulks, smokes, and writhes her way through a Millie Jackson torch song, I was ready to get down on my hands and knees and beg for it. The lady just brings out the true slut in every soul.

Tips come fast and furious, and it's curious who does the tipping. It's a very mixed crowd: straight/gay, black/white. For the female impersonators, the tipping queue includes fags, butch dykes, straight black women and me.

They also have two "masculine" stripper/dancers, à la Chippendales, who of course are gay, but perform a heterosexual romance. The straight women, black and white, line up for a mile to swoon and tip these fellas.

"What happens if a man approaches them with a tip?" I asked one of my old time companions. "He'd be ignored," was the fast reply. Now that's something I could see changed.

Why is there no female drag? Is Marlene Dietrich the only one who could ever pull it off? There have been a couple of attempts to do lesbian drag shows, but I have yet to see a male impersonator who looked like she would know what to do with a cock if she had one. There's no sense of the absolute genderfuck that the drag queens so masterfully bring to their act. Prove me wrong, please!

Are lesbian audiences ready for our own drag shows? We've only seen a couple of butch strippers at the San Francisco BurLezk. At first, only a few brave femmes would approach the stage to show their appreciation. Are lesbians afraid to show and admire their masculine selves? I'm afraid I'm going to have to sissy-bait all you pussies out there until I see some results. When are we going to learn to enjoy the sexuality of gender instead of being terrorized by it?

I couldn't say good-bye to Chicago without visiting the national headquarters of *Playboy*. *On Our Backs* photographer Honey Lee Cottrell and I marched into their downtown skyscraper at four-thirty on a Friday afternoon, confident that the employees of *Playboy* needed to know who we were.

First stop, editorial department. What a joke. The secretaries and editorial assistants we talked to revealed that they don't even look at the fleshy, sexual portions of their magazine. They're embarrassed by it.

Onto the eleventh floor, the photography department, which is clearly the guts of the magazine. Again, we saw only women working there, with the exception of one queen who came flying through the lobby, laughing, "I'm going to play consultant this week!" It's noteworthy that much of the photo work you see in *Playboy*—the covers, fashion spreads, small pictorials—is produced by a team of female editors.

Playboy's front office reception was flabbergasted by *On Our Backs*. They were particularly knocked out by the bulldagger centerfold from our first issue, and politely inquired, "There's nothing else like this, is there?"

Gosh, I was going to devote this chapter to telling you why Ben Wa balls don't work, but really, Chicago was a special sexual treat all to itself. Besides, my favorite sex toy these days is a plane ticket.

WHAT IS IT ABOUT STRAIGHT WOMEN?

FALL 1985

Oh, no, not us. Why would a lesbian be attracted to a straight woman? You don't need her anxiety, you don't need her husband, and the charm of her naiveté wears off real fast. She'll use you—but good. The Lesbian Nation doesn't need this grief.

Nevertheless, what is it about straight women? They're not everyone's kink, but the straight/gay attraction is definitely one of the most popular and enduring games in town.

The appeal of straight women is buried in mystique. Lesbians who are persistently attracted to straight women are reluctant to spell out what is so attractive to them about heterosexuals.

"Straight, my ass!" says one seasoned Lady Lover. "I've pulled more bitches out of straight bars than I ever did out of girls' bars."

"They always come on to me," another Lady Lover insists. "It's classic. She'll say, 'I never knew it could be like this...'"

"—And then leave you," chimes in another veteran. "You can always count on that."

Let's lift the swirling mist of troubled emotions that has clouded the real issue behind affairs with straight women. The truth is, straight girls can be a hot fantasy or an enduring sexual preference. We know who *they* are, but what is it about us that prompts the attraction? What kind of lesbian is a lover of straight women?

The typical Lady Lover is a Doubting Thomas. She doesn't "label" her lovers one way or the other. She claims to be non-judgmental. Despite her last seventeen consecutive affairs with straight women, she denies that their heterosexuality has anything to do with the attraction.

Well, if Ms. Thomas is too chicken to judge, we will. Her straight lovers' heterosexuality has quite a bit to do with that "uncanny" appeal. Bringing out a woman, without any doubt, is a very intoxicating experience.

There are other species in the ranks of Lady Lovers Anonymous. One is the Separatist. Every dyke who scorns heterosexual women was once, or still is, in love with them. Feminism provided a convenient set of politics with which you could dismiss straight women right out of your life. But for all the global rhetoric, the bottom line remains: She rejected you, possibly for a prick, and rejection is exquisitely bitter. You blame yourself for believing you could change her, and you'll never be fooled again. Until next time...

The real power, the real glory in store for the dedicated Lady Lover is not all this sobbing into pillows and gnashing one's teeth. The power is to accept the Straight Woman for what she is: the object of your lust. A fantasy you can masturbate over. A fling at the office, a seasonal romance. It can even be a scene you play out with a lesbian lover: "You'll be the rich straight lady leaning over the avocados in the gourmet section of Safeway, and I'll be the friendly lesbian who stares down your blouse."

In order to "come out" as a Lady Lover, it helps to articulate just what is attractive about straight women. Let's go over the basics:

1) There is nothing like a good challenge. *They* are supposedly unattainable, but *you* know your mouth and hands could make the difference. We Ladykillers experience sexual triumphs.

2) Straight women take their femininity for granted. This is particularly fascinating to lesbian butches. *They* are so utterly cool and unquashable in their womanhood, never troubled by a tomboy image or a queer's insecurity. Any Liz Taylor movie will prove this.

3) We see ourselves on a Mission of Love, as initiators of Virgins. We are delighted by their wonder and eagerness. We have so much to teach and their appetites are so enormous.

4) Straight women live outside of gay culture. Obvious, yes, but so often this is the motivation. Many a disgruntled bar dyke or burned-out lesbian activist is drawn to the woman who doesn't have a damn thing to do with us: our cliques, our habits, our hang-ups. Straight women *do* have their own hang-ups, which we don't notice at first in all the excitement.

Never let it be said that straight women are all alike. There are definite types, which in our phobia of labeling, we have never had the good sense to name.

Butch/femme terminology comes in handy here. Ordinarily, butch/femme is a description reserved for gay territory, but the same naming of style is helpful and perhaps appropriate to describe our heterosexual turn-ons.

For example, "The Doctor's Wife" is a Femme Straight Woman. She seems to have a lot of time and a lot of jewelry on her hands. She hides her vibrator from her husband, and nearly died when you put your whole hand inside her. Very thin, very clean, and she screams when she comes.

"The Roots Woman" is the Butch Straight Woman. She is surrounded by children, animals, and useless men. She's tough as nails, you feel like making a documentary out of her life, and her chest is heaven. She's never come before. You broke through her cynicism built from three alcoholic husbands. The two of you get it on in the back of the station wagon at a drive-in, while the kids are outside fighting over candy.

The list goes on. Class, race, age, and a softball team can each add endless variations. Once you have identified your straight woman fantasy as part of your erotic identity, you can truly begin to enjoy yourself. Think of her as you would any other fantasy. Do you really want to act out this fantasy, or would it lose something in the translation? Probably some experimentation will be necessary.

If straight women are definitely your sexual preference, then start appreciating the sex, instead of complaining about the limitations of the relationship. If what you love is bringing them out, why stick around to become bored and frustrated by the aftermath? If you want a vacation from the gay community, don't expect *her* to follow *our* rules.

Straight women are a lot more savvy about why they're attracted to us. We know how to kiss. We perform oral sex as a matter of course, we fuck like angels—and they never knew dry humping could be so much fun. Lesbianism is the delight of endless foreplay, foreplay with orgasms. Our skin is soft, just like theirs.

What Is It About Straight Women?

Now, you know, some straight ladies will fool you and end up becoming lesbians after all. They'll start making love back to you and come up with all kinds of little tricks that will make your clit jump up and wonder where the time went. All of a sudden, your precious, innocent straight lady will be gone. You'll find yourself instead with a real live Sapphic Wonder.

At this point, you might want to take her aside, and confess that, if the truth be known, you used to be sort of a straight woman, too.

PARTY FAVORS

WINTER 1986

How many of you have attended a home sex toy presentation with a group of friends? They're called fuckerware parties in the business, but of course they're presented much more tastefully to the public.

Your typical party caters to those who would rather die than be seen walking into a sex shop. (One woman actually told me, "What if my minister sees me?"—which sounds like one hell of a fantasy.) In many areas of the country, a sex toy party may be the only way a woman can see for herself what vibrators, dildos and g-strings are all about.

A party's success depends a lot on who's giving the presentation of the products. Nothing makes me angrier than to hear about some party representative who can barely spit out the word "clitoris" and not-so-secretly disdains the very products she's selling. Party presenters who are afraid to get sexually specific end up dwelling on lingerie and gooey chocolate stuff that you are supposed to drip all over your body in a vain attempt to get your lover to give you head.

But a good party is a place where you can find some excellent information and discussion about arousal, lubrication, orgasm, masturbation, sexual communication, erotic fantasies, and why one dildo feels better than the next.

The party rep is in the position of saying all the things that everyone else is too embarrassed to bring up. She will pass all the toys around the group to give the guests a hands-on experience. A good party takes off when the guests get beyond the "Will-I-electrocute-myself?" level and begin to share the excitement of real sexual experiences.

What do you guess is the hottest seller at sex toy parties? Lubricants! Friends, we have been facing a lubrication crisis for generations now, and it's not going to get any better. One of the first physical signs of arousal for women is vaginal lubrication. But many women find themselves uncomfortably dry when they believe they are otherwise sexually excited. Why can't we get a "wet-on" when we know we're turned on?

A number of elements in our contemporary lifestyle can dry you up even when you are aroused. Many kinds of medications, like sinus pills, will automatically dry up your vagina. The most popular recreational drugs, alcohol and marijuana, are hell on lubrication. This is an unfortunate surprise for those who think that getting high will make them hotter than ever for sex. Diet, gynecological surgery, menopause, and that favorite wild card, stress, can take all the juiciness out of your sex life. Meanwhile, sex is simply not enjoyable without lubrication, not only for penetration, but for any kind of external clit caressing.

The good news is you don't have to overhaul your whole way of life to make yourself more slippery. If you know that you're aroused and eager to make love, you can add a little dab of something slick, and presto! You are well-oiled and ready to roll.

So many women suffer the anxiety of not being lubricated enough to fuck, and wonder, "What's wrong with me *now*?" Often you'll be concerned that your lover will take offense that she isn't sexy enough to "make" you wet.

Please forget this tyranny of performance worries, and get out the proper sauce. Your lover will only be relieved to have the issue removed from preoccupation with fault. Anyone who persists in expecting you to cream your jeans every time she walks into the room is simply uninformed and not worth your precious time.

A good lubricant requires no special expense. Any vegetable oil in your kitchen will make a safe and soothing lube. Coconut oil is especially nice because it comes in a solid form and then melts luxuriously. Everything you've heard about Crisco is true—that "all vegetable oil" claim to fame makes for a splendid lubricant. Not so for animal or mineral oils. They aren't going to kill you, but they are what are called "lesion-promoting" oils which your internal tissue is not as happy with as a vegetable-based oil. Animal and mineral oil products include baby oil and all manner of lotions that you might use on your hands and face. Keep them away from your cunt!

The absolute worst is petroleum jelly. A lot of people think Vaseline is an appropriate lube because it's so often mentioned in brown-wrapper porno novels. Remember when you were a kid and grown-ups told you not to swallow chewing gum because it took seven years to digest? Well, it's the same horror story with petroleum jelly in your vagina or rectum. The stuff is not water-soluble. Water-*soluble* means that the product can be washed out and dissolved easily in water. Most oils are water soluble; petroleum jelly is not. If you can't wash it off your dishes in warm water, you won't be able to wash it out of your pussy either.

There are new kinds of water-based (non-oil) lubricants that are quite wonderful. They are extremely slick and resemble nothing so much as your own vaginal mucus. Water-based lubes are largely composed of deionized water and polymers (food grade plastic found in everything from ice cream to make-up) stretched in long molecules for true-to-life slipperiness. There are several different brands and they are safe to use; no side effects, no horrible infections or flare-ups. Check out Probe, Astroglide, and Slippery Stuff. Probe has no taste at all, and is the one I would recommend for women who are allergic to absolutely everything. Astroglide doesn't evaporate as quickly. There's a thicker type of lube called Foreplay that's sort of a souped-up K-Y jelly. The other convenient thing about water-based lubes is that they're more compatible with rubber sex toys, which tend to deteriorate when you use oils on them.

Unless you are Old Faithful, I would recommend lube every time you use dildos. Women often come to me wanting to discard a large dildo and purchase a smaller one; they confess that they cannot stuff the toy properly into their partner's or their own pussy. Dollars to donuts, the unfortunate women are not using lubricants and the results are painful and demoralizing. I would suggest that you try the same dildo again, make out with your lover until your clits are hard as rocks, apply some lube on either your vagina or the toy, and tease the dildo in. If it's still too big after a lubricated test run, then you can come back and say, "I told you so."

GET INTO THE GROUP

SPRING 1986

I promised you a full treatment on the subject of group sex and some friends have demanded *why*. Their advice: If you're trying to start a new fad, you could have picked something a little simpler.

But I have a funny feeling that most of us are actually veterans of group sex experiences, although you may have never considered them as such. Spin the Bottle is group sex. Playing Doctor is definitely a group experience, and so is parking at the drive-in or Lovers' Lane with more than one couple per car. Coming out is also a time that many women have their first uncoupled adventures. There is a whole generation of dykes who first made love with a woman as part of a ménage à trois with a man, or in answer to a swingers' advertisement. Finally, there is that hazy situation when you were going to put up Cousin Kitty on the sofa bed, but you were all so comfortable in the bedroom that one thing led to another. . .

A formal orgy, on the other hand, is something that most lesbians consider outside their experience. If we have had group sex, it was usually an unconscious sort of affair that was not discussed afterward, and certainly never planned for. There is a sense that a bona fide orgy requires either a Malibu setting complete with a water bed and patchouli oil (the sixties orgy), or perhaps leather-confident women hanging from dungeon-crafted slings or posing elbow-deep in vats of oil (the modern S/M version).

I experienced the Southern California group encounter many times as a teenager, including one where the water bed ruptured. I always liked the idea of being able to sexually connect with other people without expecting a marriage proposal the next morning.

Group sex is a playful dynamic where you can be loving without falling in love, and considerate without having to consider the consequences. It allows married couples to take a break from each other without setting up someone as the other woman. It allows you to experiment within one setting the possibilities that might take years to achieve one affair at a time.

Finally, the quintessential orgy: Many hands touching you, or your hands touching many others, is a sublime experience. Repeated exposure to group sex may rapidly convince you that it feels as natural and organically sensual as any two-person relationship. To hell with Noah's Ark!

Let's switch into Emily Post mode for a minute to talk about how to prepare the environmental ingredients for a successful group scene. Number One Hostess Tip is to invite at least twice as many people as you hope will come. R.S.V.P. is *de rigueur*. Aside from the usual sad stories about guests who drive into a ditch and don't make it, you will also find that a lot of women cop out at the last moment and spend the evening hiding in a bar, after bragging to you about how they couldn't wait to attend. Overbook and don't be sorry.

The same staples you'd expect for any good party count twice as much at a sex party. Not only does the food need to be good, it needs to be touchable. Try finger food, grapes that can be romantically peeled and slipped inside warm places, whipped cream, of course, and food that doesn't need to be hot so that you can nibble all evening. Plan for lots of beverages because this crowd is going to be thirsty.

Music is important, as are any sexy pastimes you can come up with to warm up the guests. Dancing makes people hot, and the advent of adult videos makes X-rated home entertainment a snap. There arc also some silly games you can initiate which, gimmicky as they are, will often get the ball rolling with a shy crowd. Spin the Bottle can be adapted to more sophisticated rules, and there's playing Twister in the nude, which was all the rage for a while. In general, it's not so important to get naked as it is to start the action.

There should be ready-to-romp play spaces in all the public areas. Provide soft furniture or improvise beds on the floor. Now's the time to use those satin sheets that won't stay on your bed but make for great orgy floor coverings. You should have some bottles of lubricant in strategic places, and by all means have the vibrators plugged in and the toys easy to reach.

You should be ashamed of yourself if you do not have vibrators and dildos for your guests to entertain themselves with. Even shy people are attracted to gadgets and gismos. Don't forget the rubbers and plastic gloves. Rubbers make sharing dildos easier; gloves are for the adventurous finger fuckers (as well as fist fuckers) who want to play it safe by not letting cuts and cum come into contact with each other.

What can you do at an orgy? Forget the stereotype of complicated sexual positions and being probed in every orifice all at once. Actually a well-rounded group adventure could include: watching, masturbating, facilitating someone else's pleasure, doing it to someone else, getting some yourself, or getting it all for yourself. Being a helper or a supporting actor in someone else's sex trip is a lot of fun and isn't always obvious to newcomers.

One lover of mine remembers the time she asked her friend Rita if she could lie underneath her while Rita got whipped. She got to vicariously experience S/M, which she otherwise avoids any direct contact with. Or as Rita put it, "She got the best part." Rita enjoyed the contact with a friend whom she would not ordinarily get it on with.

Sometimes our circle of friends is so incestuous it seems awkward to be intimate. I have held my best friend's head in my lap while she got fucked by four others, but I would feel uncomfortable doing it to her myself. On the other hand, in a group scene I fucked my best friend's lover, who I felt lots of affection for, but whom I never would have made it with if we hadn't had a party.

My problems with group sex are no doubt familiar to most women who've tried it:

1) shyness about how to begin;

2) asserting yourself to get what you want;

3) abandoning your inhibitions; and,

4) for those married couples in the audience, the green-eyed monster, jealousy.

What if you have the paranoia of being the "orgy virgin" who somehow ends up gangbanged by forty leather women with cocks as big as fists, all because you said "yes" when someone passed you the Crisco? Did I hear you say, "Our biggest fear is our most secret fantasy?" Yes, but sometimes one must work up to these things. I would suggest that the novice try one piece at a time rather than proving god-knows-what by attempting to entertain the whole pie. Choose one little thing that appeals to you, like watching

Deirdre get her ass licked, or vibrating yourself to a porn film while Lisa sucks your toes . . .

Ask people if you can join in. If someone invites you to sit on her face, and the act or the person doesn't attract you, consider whether you could partner with them in some other scheme that you would enjoy. Smile, shake your head, and offer something: to watch, hold the vibrator, etc. Be willing to play and participate in a cooperative frame of mind, to put yourself out a little bit, without feeling that you must say "yes" to everything that is offered you.

Letting go is easiest for the exhibitionist, and you'll find out soon enough whether you're in that category. I have been to group parties and had a great time without ever getting off. The hostess of the party usually plays the part of the gracious *grand voyeur*, although some extraordinary hosts also put themselves forward as a role model for showing how it's done. My advice: Don't worry about trying to relax. Concentrate on getting hot and the rest will follow.

Finally, the couples' ever-present thorn: jealousy. The time to deal with your guilt is before and after the party, not during. First, discuss how the two of you would be most happy attending a group event. Do both of you equally want to try this new experiment? Danger signals if one partner is more reluctant to attend than the other, and goes just to please. Some options might be to go alone, attend together with the promise of just watching, or let the reluctant partner choose a sexual activity or partner for the more interested one.

Decide if you want to split up and not be involved with each other at all, or if the object is to stay together and solicit partners as a couple. It's essential to discuss the guidelines and limits before you go, and refrain from pressuring your partner to do something not agreed upon prior to the party. If something comes up that you would like to do, discuss it with your partner and save it for the next time.

If you think you might boil over despite your best intentions, just make sure you have cab fare home, and make a discreet exit. Group scenes are *not* encounter groups, make no mistake. The best thing you can do for your relationship is to plan a special brunch or leisurely walk the next day to discuss your feelings and the events that took place. And remember, sometimes the best way to soothe possessive or guilty feelings is to share an incredibly hot fuck with your lover later.

Are you ready to send out the invitations now? Can I bring my inflatable doll? You can be sure of an R.S.V.P. from me.

RUB-A-DUB GUMBO

FALL 1986

*C*hère, I am just back from the French Quarter and the funniest things seem to make sense. I had only the tiniest taste of New Orleans during the weekend I spent there, but it was also one of the sweetest.

Officially, I was in Louisiana for the American Bookseller's Convention (ABA), where all your neighborhood bookshop people rendezvous with every publisher in the business. I was working for Down There Press, which clearly had the best button of the convention: "A Whole Book About What?—*Anal Pleasure and Health.*"

Unofficially, the theme of this year's ABA was censorship. I was floored to hear censorship horror stories about *Penthouse*, astrology books, and *On Our Backs* all from the same store! The owner of that very progressive bookshop arrived one morning to find his windows painted "This Store Promotes Violence Against Women." Later in the afternoon a hellfire-and-brimstone mother threatened to sue the store for "making my son into a homosexual." Then in came a group of "concerned citizens" who purportedly wanted *Playboy* off the shelves, but when pressed for details, revealed that they also wanted all the astrology, tarot, and Eastern religion books out the door, too.

The bookshop clerk pleaded, "But our store provides a whole body of spiritual literature; we even have several versions of the Christian Bible."

Concerned Citizens were not impressed. They quoted: "There is only *one* Bible."

And to ice the cake, a local feminist author, who was scheduled for a special appearance, said she wouldn't attend unless *On Our Backs* and other sexually explicit lit was taken off the shelves. Hey—I bet she's got *one* Bible, too!

Ladies, I didn't know whether to throw up or throw punches. Put all censors on notice that I consider their efforts totalitarian piggery, and their horror of explicit sexuality a thin veneer for their own ignorance and hypocritical morality.

In contrast to the hubbub in the convention center, New Orleans was a luxurious bath of eroticism. Society there does not have a work ethic; they have a pleasure ethic. Gay life is a perfect example, although lots of women complained to me of the stifling atmosphere and racial segregation (gee, we wouldn't know about that in California). I heard, "I'm the only leather dyke in town," and "That's the South for you." The gay ghetto is thriving, but it remains much to itself, and those who are out of the closet are that way because they never leave the Quarter.

The silver lining to this phenomenon is that you do feel like you are entering a magical city within a city. Once a year, the magic takes over and queerness reigns supreme.

Rub-A-Dub Gumbo

Mardi Gras is the ultimate genderfuck holiday. The rest of the year, the community plans for Mardi Gras, or, in any case, never completely gets off the social wheel of parties, picnics, raffles, and special services. I have no idea how any work gets done around here. There are the bars, and then there are the gay churches, and they rule the roost between them. One woman remarked how New Orleans bartenders serve as the role models and gay community leaders, which gave me a big laugh, but I'm sure it's true.

Charlene's is one of the oldest and best known places in town, and I thought the owner, Charlene herself, was a pearl to bring a cold bucket of champagne to the gay bookshop opening that featured myself and two Naiad Press authors as special guests.

My favorite person in New Orleans (I hope I don't get in trouble for saying it) was Brenda Laura, who recently took over the old Pinos bar. The night I met her she was hosting the gay ABA party at her club. She had on a red silk dress, red velvet pumps with little jewels on them, and the most extraordinary gold pendant around her neck. It was a little figurine of a naked woman on a swing with a diamond shining right where her clit would be. Of course, I had to inquire about this little item. Brenda asked me if I'd been down Bourbon Street yet, which is the party avenue and features several strip shows. One burlesque house has a facade where a pair of papier-maché naked ladies' legs swing out over your head from an opening in their awning, while the sound of laughter and tinkling glasses plays in the background. This Venus in a Swing was the inspiration of Ms. Laura's pendant. Need I say more?

The best club I went to was the Country Club, a big ol' southern mansion overtaken by vines and blossoms, with a porch swing on the veranda. Two of the rooms inside were furnished as bars. One had a rack of sexy boys' magazines, and I stuck in a few *On Our Backs* for good measure. The other rooms were for lounging or dancing. At the back you entered an enormous garden, with a huge play pool, hot tub, locker, and a weight room. Beware Yankee, this is not a yuppie spa! It was dilapidated and funky like every other antique location in New Orleans, hotter than hell, and with cockroaches as long as your fingers. I loved every minute of it.

I have another salty adventure about attending the Harlequin Romance company party, dancing with girls there and discovering one of them is a Fort Lauderdale subscriber to *On Our Backs*. She was there marketing a book called *101 Uses for an Ex-Husband*. We are everywhere, all right.

One Harlequin Romance executive approached me mid-waltz, my latest issue in his hand, and asked, "What is this word *tri-bid-ism*?" So glad he asked!

I've wanted to talk about tribadism for a while now, because so many of you practice this ancient Sapphic activity but don't know what the word is. Straight teenagers have their own term for it, expressed in their anguish at not going all the way: dry humping. I've heard some queens refer to the same action as *frottage*. But for lesbians, our little mounds are just made for rubbing up against each other, and this passion is known as *tribad-*(rhymes with livid)-*ism*.

Most of us have read torrid accounts of tribadism in those great old pulp novels about dykes. Here's a passage from one of my favorites, circa 1960, *Lesbian Hell*, by Jane Sherman:

Betty had educated hips. She pushed them against

me and twisted rhythmically until I thought I'd flip. I wanted her to wait for it. She'd like it better that way. She was bruising my body with those over-active hips of hers. Betty was a healthy girl; she pushed up against me like she loved the rough stuff. "Give it to me baby, give it to me," Betty breathed. We were making it together in perfect harmony. I wanted to become part of her, make her part of me.

This lusty excerpt actually has some great facts about tribadism. Being face to face, full bodies facing each other, makes for a "melding" intimacy that no other position affords you. However, you can do tribadism on your lover's tail bone, forearm or knee—any part of her that your cunt can get a good angle on.

Tribadism is also a successful method for simultaneous climaxes. Like the book said, it's all in the rhythm, and you definitely have to practice to get your rubbing "in perfect harmony." How much practice? It seems like when you've got a hot affair going, time flies, and you can get this type of thing synchronized within a month.

Some women don't orgasm through tribadism because it doesn't give them enough direct clitoral stimulation, and still leaves their mons sore and bruised in the morning. Here is a fun and easy way to cheat: use a vibrator, the wand type, between yourself and your lover. The little vibrating tennis ball-type heads are just *made* to go between lesbians' thighs. You still get a lot of body contact with your lover, but it's easier to find a common point of stimulation.

I have a theory about why tribadism is so rarely talked about. It's a full body embrace that departs from hugging, and turns it into an erotic technique. Tribadism can be accomplished without many words, without looking, tasting, or touching your genitals, without even taking your clothes off. As such, it has a special appeal for people who are embarrassed about their bodies, pussies in particular, and lesbian lovemaking in general. There's something historically furtive about tribadism, as if it were something you do without acknowledging that you're really having S-E-X.

One last post-feminist angle to this secretiveness is that some women feel guilty about tribadism because it reminds them of the heterosexual missionary position, and they get uptight about who's on the bottom and who's on top. I'll reiterate once again that the only people who are more hung up about penis/vagina sex than straight men are guilty lesbians. Believe me, whether you're on top or bottom, you have to do your share of the rhythm or the tribadism won't work.

Obviously, there are plenty of lesbians who use tribadism as one of many sexual activities they enjoy. It is not a secret, closeted practice by nature. In fact, it's pretty hard to avoid some arousing bone-to-clit rubbing if you have a varied sex life. By the way, tribadism can swing either way as an S/M technique or vanilla style. Read the rest of *Lesbian Hell* and I think you'll figure it out.

I've got one last bit of white trash advice to dole out. A southern sister from the state of Georgia, lamenting the ban on vibrators and dildos in that state (censorship moves fast if you don't cut its head off), wrote to Good Vibrations and told us that every country girl worth her salt had a sincere cucumber patch thriving in the back yard. No, these cucumber devotees are not especially interested in funny tasting pickles. We're talking a serious, seasonal dildo collection.

Pay attention to these growing tips from Ellie Mae:
"1) Don't use sprays on the cucumber plant, ever;

2) Sometimes the premature cucumber skin will act like poison ivy, so if you are allergic to poison ivy, by all means let the cucumber ripen before you use it;

3) Beware store-bought cucumbers—wash 'em real good. (I soak store-bought cukes in douche);

4) Set a cuke outside in the hot sun for a day to make it flexible. Don't peel it until ready to use!"

Thank you for sharing, sister. You'll excuse me now if I go pickle myself.

A HAND IN THE BUSH

WINTER 1987

One of the great misunderstood characters of the world is the lesbian fist fucker. Her sexual technique of inserting her whole hand in her lover's cunt is considered physically impossible by some, and bizarre to others. To those uninitiated to the pleasures of handballing, I invite you to study this column thoroughly. Don't be ashamed of your sexual illiteracy, just remedy it. For those of you who are veteran pussy handlers, grab your lube, because we're about to go public.

Fisting, if you had to compare it to anything else, is a natural extension of finger fucking. One day your cunt is hungrier than usual, and three fingers just aren't enough. Not four or five, either. At that point, some lovers will opt for their favorite dildo. But the drawback with dildos is the lack of flesh-to-flesh contact. Putting your curled-up hand in your lover's vagina won't give you direct clitoral stimulation, but it will give you direct hormonal stimulation. The intimacy is unbelievable. You are all the way inside of your lover; her body is wrapped around your fist like a cocoon. You can feel every tremor originating from her cunt, her ass, and her womb—and she can feel every tiny movement your fingers make. Just twisting your wrist is like the earth moving inside her. If this sounds romantic, you're right. Fisting is incredibly romantic.

If you get aroused through vaginal penetration, you will like being fisted. But if you have never been truly thrilled by fucking, fisting may turn the key. If you are partial to mind-shattering orgasms, fisting is a one-way ticket. If you always wanted to have a girl in the palm of your hand—well, here you go.

Now that we've established the pleasure principle, let's look at some of the misunderstandings.

Vaginal fisting is a whole different activity than anal fisting. The lining of your anus and rectum are very delicate, and while the vagina is not made of steel, it is a tough old broad by comparison.

The anxiety about anal sex often focuses on the possibility of infecting a cut or scratch with feces, but the vagina presents a completely different environment. What this means is that some of the precautions one would normally take with any kind of ass fucking are not relevant to vaginal fisting. It is not necessary to cut and file your fingernails to touch a cunt. It's common sense to keep your claws curled under, whether you're using one finger or five. Wash your little paws like any decent girl would, and if you're worried about infection, or your fingertips getting pruny from the wet heat of your lover's cunt, use a pair of surgical gloves. They're thin enough that you can feel everything, and yet you'll both be protected.

Another myth is that fisting is an S/M activity. Please. Anything can be eroticized by an S/M approach or attitude, but simply lying back and taking it does not make one a "bottom" any more than fucking your lover makes you a "top." A fisting has more in common with petting below the waist than it does with a good whipping. If you're experiencing pain during fist fucking, *stop!* You're doing it wrong.

Do you have enough lubrication? Your lubrication level is easily assisted by a good oil or jelly. I've never heard of a successful fisting that didn't include plenty of your favorite lubricant. Is your cervix too sensitive to take any rough bumping or prodding? Your cervix/uterus sensitivity will vary with the time of your menstrual cycle, and the degree of arousal.

In order to insert your hand in your lover, she needs to be aroused and hungry to be fucked. When she is physically stimulated enough to receive your fist, her vagina will be dilated. The upper section will swell like a balloon, while the lower entrance to her cunt will lengthen and grow puffy with vasocongestion. The time is ripe.

Press in one finger at a time, until they're all immersed up to your bottom knuckles. Keep playing with her clit, or nipples, or whatever hot places she likes to be touched. Now you're ready for the crucial *push* to get past your knuckles and see your whole hand go inside. For some women that will feel like a slow, steady push; for others, like a "pop" followed by a swallow. Once inside, your hand will naturally curl under into a ball to accommodate the snug, elastic space you've created.

Some women don't believe that they could ever be able to handle the size of a fist inside of them. I hear comments like, "Only women with extra large vaginas can take a fisting." Or, "You need to have gone through childbirth to do that." Horse feathers.

Vaginas, unlike ready-to-wear, do not come in rigid sizes, small, medium, and large. Each woman's vagina comes with the capability to deliver a baby, which is larger than any fist you're likely to come across. So why do women seem to have so many differences when it comes to how much penetration they can enjoy?

There are some women whose vaginal openings are so tight they cannot take any hint of penetration without pain. This is called *vaginismus*, and the term is usually reserved for extreme situations. Vaginismus is an inability to relax vaginal muscles, stemming from a woman's fear of being hurt through penetration. It is not a physical disability. If we anesthetized such a woman, her vaginal opening would relax. It's this fear of taking things into our cunts, our mouths or our assholes that results in the protective reaction of closing up.

Telling your muscles to relax is no small trick. First you have to convince yourself that you won't get hurt, and then you have to have some pleasurable experiences to back up that perception. Many women have accustomed themselves to a certain size dildo or number of fingers, but they could just as well become familiar with a lover's hand. The experience of childbirth does not make your vagina larger, it simply convinces the laboring mother that such pussy elasticity is possible.

There is also apprehension on the part of the woman who's doing the fisting. "What if I can't get my hand out?" she may ask, imagining her lover's cunt like a vice-grip around her wrist.

Never fear, Romeo, your hand will see the light of day again. That tightening you feel is the vagina lengthening and swelling, creating an orgasmic platform that you could feel with your fingers if it wasn't already squeezing around your bracelet. She's going to come any minute now, and when she does, you will feel every contraction as if it were your own, and afterwards her vagina will relax and you will be able to ease your hand out.

A Hand in the Bush

I have one friend who had the unique experience of fisting two women at the same time, one hand in each pussy. Each woman reacted very differently to the fucking, and one found it quite painful. What was the matter? Just because you have successfully fisted one partner, you do not necessarily have a road map to every woman's cunt. It's very unlikely that each woman being fisted would be identically aroused, with their vaginas dilated to exactly the same degree at the same time. Imagine trying to blow up two balloons to exactly the same size. Your only path to be a double-fisted wonder is to keep each hand in a special rhythm tuned to each woman's tempo. Syncopation? It sounds like it would be worth the trouble.

CRIMES AGAINST NATURE

SUMMER 1987

Forget Oliver North. Forget the shopping mall ter-rorists, the muggers, the pickpockets, and the crim-inally insane.

There's a new crime wave sweeping the country and not one local news program has the guts to cover it: sex toy vandalism. My phone has become a hotline of sorts for hysterical victims whose harnesses have been pinched, and whose rubber novelties have been mutilated.

Just last night a dear friend called to say that she and her lover had their camping trip ruined when someone entered their tent and snatched their black bag full of sex toys: one hundred and fifty dollars worth, she said, not an uncommon price for a vibrator, dildo, harness, and lube.

My friends did the gutsy and right thing—they indig-nantly reported their loss to the park ranger. Might he be a suspect? These vicious robberies are terribly under-re-ported, but the problem isn't going to go away by keeping it a secret.

My advice? Especially at the big parks like Grand Canyon and Yellowstone, keep your dildo strapped on at all times, and your vibrator attached to your canteen belt or day pack. You'll have more fun in the forest and you won't have any nagging worries about what's going down at base camp.

The other type of sex gadget vandalism I hear about is usually committed by someone you know very well—like an ex or soon-to-be ex-lover. I'd like a show of hands as to how many of you have watched in horror as your girlfriend picked up a butcher knife and hacked your rubber dick into a million pieces. Or worse, she's done the dirty deed in private and then stuffed the remains into your pillowcase or the soles of your shoes. It's the kind of act that initially invites laughter, but when you consider the prices we pay for these items, the humor quickly fades.

The partner who had the guts to walk into the sleazy adult store in the first place to buy the precious item is usually not the one who wrecks the toy. It seems that with a lot of couples, one partner stays in the car chewing her nails while the other one attempts to look like she knows what she's doing as she tiptoes into Bob's Fantasy Fun Palace.

There is no reason why you shouldn't get to know your own local novelty store. "Bob" at the Fantasy Palace is no more threatening than the sales clerk at Woolworth's, and no one is going to make a pass at you.

The male customers in the store are more afraid of you than you are of them. Watch them cut a wide swath to get out of your way as you head toward the tit clamps. It's an awesome sense of power. I don't know why men can be so rude at a bus stop but then be absolutely speechless in a sex toy store, but that's the way it is.

Back to the problem of inter-relationship dildo abuse.

Thwarting such expensive destruction takes more sensitivity and imagination than the vacation rip-off cases.

First off, consider whether you or your lover have ·a secret pent up desire to carve up a dildo. The urge has a certain free-for-all cachet to it, like spraying whip cream everywhere, or jumping off the high diving board. It's perfectly legitimate to have these cravings, but don't wait for a temper tantrum to act them out. Go buy one of those eight dollar monster jobs today, and the next time you feel mischievous or eager to act out your intense hatred of your boss, your father, or the IRS, just haul out Mr. Dong and show that rubber what it's made for. You'll have saved yourself an expensive and needless therapy session.

The intimate toys you really care about, however, deserve the same material respect you'd give to a gold lamé evening gown or a new motorcycle. Some of you married or semi-married girls are courting trouble by sharing the dildo outside of your primary relationship. At the very least, you should be using condoms if you care at all about your friends' and your own health. If you think there might be some jealous reactions as well, leave the marriage trophy at home and buy yourself an extra swinger model.

And speaking of that all important shopping trip. . . I've seen so many new lesbian couples come into Good Vibrations, fresh from the jewelry and linen departments at Macy's, who are making that special intimate decision together: Shall we get the lavender, or the flesh tone?

Six months to a year later, one half of the couple returns, usually with a new haircut, but always recognizable to my discerning eyes. She admits with a sigh or a grunt that her other half has flown the coop, and with her went the Hitachi, the butt plug, and assorted ostrich feathers.

What can you say in these cases except *c'est la vie*? While some nervous or jaded lovers decide right off the bat who's buying and owning what, developing a philosophical attitude towards new romance seems only to result from paying your dues. (Please pass the Kleenex.)

If we were all rich, we could afford to be more capricious, but your average lesbian, who's trying to pose as a yuppie on a shoestring income, would do better to hold back that Visa card in the first bloom of lust. You don't want to be paying nineteen and a half percent interest on the dildo that got away.

DAM IT, JANET!

FALL 1987

When I bring up safe sex, most lesbians make a face like someone pushed a bowl of cold spinach in front of them. I have a very different point of view about safe sex: I see it as an introduction to sexual variation that will last long after the AIDS epidemic. After all, if you learn a new way to become aroused and get off like you never dreamed of before, you're not going to turn in your nouveau methods just because someone comes out with a vaccine.

Some sex we've been doing all along is "safe": tribadism and vibrators, for example.

But I would like to get to the heart of the least understood safe sex accessories: condoms, rubber gloves, and the elusive dental dams.

Condoms are the biggest convenience item since disposable dixie cups. Anyone who has ever shared a dildo or vibrator knows how easy it is to pass a yeast infection, let alone herpes or AIDS. Usually we get out of bed and wash our toys between uses. But you can keep condoms on the night table next to your lubricant, and roll one right over your rubber ducky at a moment's notice. When you switch the toy into another orifice, you simply strip off that rubber and slide on another one. No muss, no fuss, no getting out of bed, and no boiling dildos in your spaghetti pot!

When I recently demonstrated rubber gloves in Denver, a couple of women in the audience flushed bright red as soon as I slipped one on my hand. They obviously have had the slick, smooth, delicious experience of being fucked by a gloved hand. The latex is so sensitive that the wearer feels every bit of heat and wetness while the receiver gets all the pressure without any scratches or rough edges. When I've used latex for finger or fist fucking, I've been amazed to extract my hand from the glove and find it dry—the lubrication felt so close to me. What I love, as a chronic nail biter, is that my lover's juices don't sting my hands anymore. No more pruny fingertips! Suffice to say, I will always enjoy using latex glove wear.

Now the item that everyone is so uptight about: latex dental dams. Well, I'm about to set your wig straight once and for all. Dams are not only easy to orgasm with in the traditional manner (Cunnilingus 101), but you can pursue oral delights you never conceived of before, thanks to this little four-by-five inch square of sexual satisfaction.

Gourmet technique number one is a special clitoral vacuum suck. Stretch a dam over your lover's clit. Feel with your tongue until you can sense her head and foreskin. Now purse your lips around that tiny area and suck in a minuscule bubble of rubber. This will make a nice little vacuum effect on the clit underneath. You can actually "suck bubbles" all over, but as a fan of direct stimulation, I like the clit bubble the best.

The secret about dams is that their true liberating effect is for anal sex. With a dam in place, you can approach rimming with the same gusto that you would ordinarily reserve for kissing babies.

It's interesting to me that the typical sex manuals always recommend enemas and thorough cleansing before analingus. But in real life, pre-AIDS, most people either avoided eating shit by *never* getting their mouths near anyone's ass, or they resigned themselves to taking a small risk while enjoying the benefits of all that soft, hot tonguing that every anus craves. Nowadays, with the more frightening prospect of AIDS, most people have sworn off rimming unless they are in long term monogamous relationships.

Enter the dental dam. With dams, you can skip the hour-long shower, forget the Fleet enema, can the monogamy and simply throw your inhibitions in the trash! With a latex square over your lover's anus, you can lick, munch, and probe to your healthful heart's content.

I've saved the best for last.

Ever since I was in Sex Ed Kindergarten, I've been warned that one must never move her mouth from the anus to the vulva, risking infection. Wrong Way. No Entrance. Like a good girl, I adapted my sexual habits to avoid this taboo two-step.

But imagine this: with a latex dam stretched vertically from the anus to vagina, you can happily take one long lick from bottom to top, without flinching. It feels great! You can't believe you're getting away with it! You can't believe this is called Safe Sex!

Yes, there is a silver lining to the STD epidemic, and it comes in mint flavors, too. Long live latex.

FISTING TWO

WINTER 1988

Oh, sodomy. . . It doesn't come naturally just because you're gay. We stumble and fumble and watch dirty movies for tips, but there's a lot to lesbian sex that doesn't get talked about. I recently had the pleasure of hosting a hands-on lesbian fist fucking workshop in Seattle, during the 1987 Living In Leather conference.

Such an outrageous subject required a little extra work. LaMar, a Seattle tattoo artist, promised me a real doctor's examination table. I took out a classified ad in the *Seattle Gay News*, to recruit "vaginally able volunteers" for participants. I got a couple of crank calls, but one diamond. A woman named Donna said that she and her lover were fisting gourmets, and she would be happy to be my guinea pig.

I was nervous about meeting Donna in person. I wanted to do a brief, private rehearsal with her before the main event, but how was I to ask? "Excuse me, but shall we do this privately one time to make sure that I can get in and out of your cunt?"

I put on my best Susie Sexpert manners and suggested we talk about all the details first, which proved to be invaluable. Unlike some women whose favorite fisting movement is a slow clenching and unclenching, Donna preferred more circular massage motions. She showed me where to put extra lubrication around my gloved hand. When we got closer to our trial run, I suggested she bring her lover, Carrie, for bedside reassurance. Our rehearsal went smooth as silk.

The next afternoon, sixty women crammed into a small airless room for the Vaginal Fisting Workshop. The tension was so thick you could have wired your home with it. First I passed out my rubber gloves, condoms and dams, with a few words on safe sex techniques. Rubber or vinyl gloves are really superior for fisting over naked hands. They grease up better and give a smoother surface going in.

I asked who in the room had read my original essay on fisting, and to my amazement, every woman raised her hand. I explained that I wanted to hear about others' experiences with all the details of fisting. Why do we like fisting? Does it ever hurt, and why? What are the effects of drugs, surgery, other health problems? Is there fisting performance anxiety? Does fisting always lead to orgasm?

A couple women complained that some lovers they fisted wanted to be fucked too hard, and they were worried that they were going to hurt their partners.

Just as there seemed to be a consensus against rough fucks, a brave soul spoke up. "I like getting fisted hard; I like my cervix getting bumped. Sometimes I spot (menstrual blood) the next day, and I used to worry whether I was hurting myself, but I don't experience any other symptoms."

That drew a pause. This is simply something you can't ask your doctor, not only because you're embarrassed, but because the damn doctor doesn't know anything about it! We discussed what we know about the sensitivity of the cervix. Bruising or pressure isn't necessarily harmful, but prodding or piercing the cervical opening (the os) is dangerous, and obviously not what fisting is all about.

Another woman brought up that the peril isn't necessarily for the *fistee*, it's for the *fister*. She once had a lover orgasm while her hand was curled up inside, and the contractions broke a small bone in her hand! Her experience prompted a lot of handy hints on how to get out of a woman's cunt in a hurry when your hand is caught in a vacuum. Methods include pressing gently on her lower abdomen, or using a finger on your free hand to pull a little on the vaginal opening, thereby breaking the suction. Simply relaxing until her muscles loosen is the simplest method. Don't panic, or you'll have a funny time telling people why your hand is in a splint.

We moved onto orgasm. My experience with being fisted is that sometimes I feel like I'm on a long dreamy hard ride, which produces a meditative feeling, but not the high pitch that would lead toward orgasm. It's such a powerful feeling that I'm not unsatisfied and occasionally I'm surprised to end up climaxing after all.

Other lesbians in the workshop said this was true for them as well. The conversation turned to a discussion of orgasms. We discovered that just because you're not orgasm-oriented doesn't mean that you aren't hungry to reach other goals.

There were lots of other stories: women who can't get fisted reliably and feel humiliated when they can't open up, and lovers who say that their girlfriends complain that they aren't trying hard enough to fist them, but who feel like they will injure their partner or do something stupid if they force it. (True.) It is awful when fisting becomes a tribute of lust that you have to *prove* to someone, just as many of us have felt compelled to orgasm "in the right way, at the right time" in order to prove our sexual prowess. Those kind of attitudes are paralyzing!

Finally one woman said, "I'm tiny and proud. I've never been fisted, but I do enjoy fucking, and if it ever happens, that's fine. I'm not losing sleep over it. I also enjoy fisting my lovers, which is why I'm here today."

It was time to slide out the examination table. Donna climbed on top, sans hospital sheet, and Carrie cosied up on her left. I squirted the last of my non-oxynol lube into my gloved palm, and was so excited that I waved my hand and splattered half of it on the audience. I started playing with the outside of Donna's pussy, telling everyone what we had discussed the night before, and how helpful it was to have an explicit conversation before getting it on. Soon I had all my fingers and thumb up to my big knuckles inside her. With one quick motion I was inside of her up to my wrist.

I abruptly stopped my lecture and realized how hot the the room was: the red faces, stillness where there had been constant chatter before, all eyes intent on watching my hand move in and out. I think if I had kept it up any longer we might have had an orgy, but more likely we'd have run out of oxygen.

"I'm going to come out now, okay? Will somebody open up that door before we all pass out?"

Donna stood up, and we applauded each other. I started packing up my rubber utensils. It was hard to leave. Women kept coming up, telling me it was the best lesbian event they'd ever been to. I felt the same way.

"What exactly did you like so much about it?" I asked.

The answer came from Lainie, also a facilitator at the conference. "What I liked the best was having an actual lesbian perform an actual act of penetration." That about sums it up. I'm pleased that fisting, the most secretive of all our activities, is bringing up sexual issues that lesbians are experts on.

HOW TO STUFF A WILD LESBIAN BIKINI:

A Survey of Contemporary Lesbian Sexual Fiction

SPRING 1988

We have reached the point of no return. Over the past ten years, we have witnessed a coming out party for lesbian erotic literature. If the genre is not yet mature, these debutantes have still affected the rest of the lesbian fiction market so thoroughly that readers simply will not find a new dyke novel that doesn't take a well-meaning stab at a lesbian sex scene.

Let's not make any "ifs" about it—lesbian erotica, in book form, is far from mature, far from eloquent, and many orgasms away from being completely captivating. Yet, because lesbian erotic novels and anthologies are still so rare, each volume is fascinating. Even the very worst writing is an insight into lesbian sexual consciousness.

The new lesbian pornographers have produced a wave of modern lesbian literature that challenges the notion of noble passivity, the beautiful anguish we've been smothered by ever since *The Well of Loneliness*. For this we are grateful.

Since we are still in the "new bride" period, lesbian readers must first define what the hell they expect from the new sexual fiction. My definitions will hopefully be of assistance:

Erotica is *not* meant to reassure you that you are normal, or that homosexuality is a marvelous, natural thing. Erotica *is* about escapism, into those secret feelings that, romantically enough, no one but you understands.

Erotica is *not* about feeling smug; it *is* about feeling aroused. Clearly, the first test for erotic literature is: Did you come? Were you excited enough to turn your reading into a one-handed affair, or did you rush off to find your lover? Did you squeeze your thighs together and make yourself wet?

Lesbian erotica is not about beautiful people lolling about with beautiful clothes and beautiful smiles. It *is* about unlikely characters, unique situations and plenty of conflict leading up to the big bang. It's about personal taste, and the sensitivity to crave someone or something that maybe the whole world won't appreciate. Erotica is not Wonder Bread, although it can be a Hostess Snowball.

Good erotica is not technical writing. It does not teach you how to perform cunnilingus, ass fucking, or stand-up tribadism. Erotica can be detailed, and it's often explicit, but it does not exist to tell you what the left hand is doing five inches over the right tit. In good porn you feel every move, but it's seamless; the author has greased you in, and you didn't even know what happened.

Those who believe in erotica with a capital *E* will announce that Eroticism is far more than "mere" orgasm. Look, *turning on* is the bottom line. When you relish a story physically *and* experience it as lyrical, unforgettable, transformational—well, you've got a literary masterpiece on your hands.

It's so hard to write a good sex scene. Our language is impoverished when it comes to an erotic vocabulary. Tee Corinne says that one of the main motivations for writing her *Dreams of the Woman Who Loved Sex* was to expand erotic language, to combine the medical terminology with street slang, as well as add her own metaphors and other original contributions.

It's still tough. The first year I edited *On Our Backs*, I insisted that we would not print a single story that used the "ocean" as an orgasmic metaphor. Nor would I print any seashell pictures. We have been discouraged by sexual clichés, and yet the best pornographers manage to make those clichés come alive. How do they do it?

Like any expert storyteller, skilled erotica authors build believable, if outrageous, characters. They employ cinematic timing, and then just when the reader's breath begins to hold back, they sock her with a cornball line or dirty word that would never work in a million years—except that by this point, she's so vulnerable she's dying for it.

The best examples of this, after all these years, are the original lesbian pulps from the fifties. No one can beat Ann Bannon's *Women in the Shadows*, *Odd Girl Out*, *I Am a Woman*, *Journey to a Woman*, *Beebo Brinker* (reissued by Naiad Press) for inexplicit, yet undeniably sweaty eroticism:

Laura felt such a wave of passion come up in her that it almost smothered her. She thought she couldn't stand it. She only clung to Beebo, half tearing her pajamas off her back, groaning wordlessly, almost sobbing.

Out of context, this excerpt may scream "kitsch," but after the first twenty pages of *I Am a Woman*, the reader is sobbing to tear those pajamas off herself. When Naiad re-issued Bannon's classics in 1983, they were a smash, especially with the new generation of young lesbians who were desperate for real descriptions of bar life, butch/femme style, down and dirty serial monogamy—all of which had been blacked out by the lesbian feminist press of the seventies.

Nowadays, we have a contemporary roster of lesbian pulps coming from Naiad, but few can be classified as erotica. Katherine Forrest, whose 1983 novel, *Curious Wine*, proved that even the most conservative lesbians were longing for juicy love scenes, has led the pack of gay girl Harlequins. But honestly, the modern crop of Naiad romances make Harlequin look risqué.

Lace Publications, the imprint of author Artemis Oakgrove, is the largest press specializing in lesbian sex. Oakgrove has published her own S/M novels, the *Throne Trilogy*, an erotic anthology, *The Leading Edge*, and books by Regine Sands, *Travels With Diana Hunter*, and other authors.

Oakgrove's success proves that there is a market for hardcore lesbian novels. She is utterly unconcerned with what anybody in the feminist literary elite thinks and shamelessly plunders stereotypes and sexual clichés. Because she possesses a dedicated, no-holds-barred vision of what turns her on, she can grind out S/M bodice-rippers like a kinky Barbara Cartland. She's not as good a writer as Cartland though. Sometimes the prose is plain dreadful, but her fantasies are suspiciously on the mark. They're the kind of books you skim to find the "good parts," and Artemis always delivers.

No one knows how to critique her writing. The traditional critics are embarrassed by her craft, and they use that as an excuse to avoid talking about the sexual taboos she speaks of so blatantly. In her latest novel, *Nighthawk*, a ditzy voluptuous blonde finds herself stranded in a rough ghetto billiard room, where she is unceremoniously stripped by the meanest black butch in the place, and gang banged by the rest:

> Lori froze. She knew what a big stick like that could do if she fought against it—it could rip her wide open. She knew only too well. Lori was twenty-one years old but she had already lost her uterus because Cloud had gone crazy one night and wouldn't listen when she begged her to stop.

If this isn't plain-brown-wrapper reading, I don't know what is. It has no careful intellect, no political sensitivity, no historical basis. I wish someone *would* write about rape fantasies, gang bangs, and inter-racial sex confrontations with social insight *and* salaciousness. But those who could, won't. They won't risk their precious literary reputations. Oakgrove has no literary reputation to defend, but she has guts: the first qualifier for an author of lesbian sexual fiction.

Next on the shelf, we have the lesbian self-publishers and selections from erotic anthologies. Anthologies have been the bane of women's erotic publishing, because other than Lace, no publisher has taken the risk of printing an entire novel about one woman's erotic preference. By offering a potpourri, anthology editors hope to cast a wide net, and at least offer good reading and insight with all their selections, even if only one or two turn on an individual reader. This is a fine goal, but it still smells of the poverty of women's publishing.

The most famous new anthologies are Lonnie Barbach's *Pleasures* and *Erotic Interludes*, which each have a sprinkling of lesbian couples. I wouldn't mind scarcity so much if it weren't for the content. All the gay women in these stories are such Girl Scouts! They dream of getting it on, but never do; they hold themselves back for higher purposes. They're so fucking lofty you wonder if they can reach down low enough to pull their pants off. The only lesbian tale from either collection that sticks in my mind is "The Ditchdigger" by Tee Corrine. Corrine gets in the mud with an elegant description of how country dykes accomplish hard work and gentle loving in the same day.

The most unusual and underground lesbian sex novel is *Bizarro in Love*, self-published by Jan Stafford. Stafford owes her inspiration not to any lesbian feminist pioneers or S/M dungeon, but to Janis Joplin.

Who remembers that best-of-all unauthorized star biography, *Going Down With Janis*, by Peggy Caserta (as told to Don Knapp)? Let me refresh you with the first paragraph:

> I was stark naked, stoned out of my mind on heroin, and the girl lying between my legs giving me head was Janis Joplin. She was stoned blind on smack, too, but the junk flowing through her veins hadn't diminished the skill with which she used her mouth on me.

Now, *Bizarro* is not about rock and roll, but rather the story of an obsessed sports writer who makes it with everyone from movie star tennis champs to a Southern U cheerleader. Her tie to Janis Joplin is that she does not hesitate to combine the drug experience with the sex experience:

> She copped two grams of coke at Mission and Sixth and snorted in the bathroom of the Greyhound Bus terminal. The rush hit her like a brick orgasm. As she exited the terminal even the winos looked like archangels. It wasn't hard for Bizarro to pick up the first available dyke cruising in the front of the Civic Center Hotel. . .
>
> The numbing effect of the drug made them comfortable in any position. They remained locked in a licking embrace for hours. Bizarro nodded out. When she awoke, her partner was kneeling in front of her wearing a dildo that seemed to have no end. "You ain't seen nothing yet," said the dyke. She pressed a button and the big thing vibrated and swirled in a circular motion.

Bizarro is more comic than it is arousing, and like other oddballs in the lesbian erotic bookshelf, it's more notable as lesbian history than as classic erotica.

So what *is* classic? The frustrating state of affairs is that the very hottest, most brilliant lesbian sexual fiction has nearly all been published as short stories in periodicals, with the occasional gem found in an anthology. Here we find prose that is not only titillating, but delights in being read out loud. Classic erotic stories surprise; they touch the unconscious. For the dedicated reader, there is no choice but to dig up all the back issues and anthologies, and put together a loose leaf binder of the very best in lesbian erotica. I have my own personal favorites I simply would not exist on a desert island without.

The Island 15

Or, Susie Sexpert's Favorite Escapist Lesbian Sex Stories

1) "The Telephone" by Martha Courtot, *On Our Backs*, Spring 1985. Dial M for Magnificent suspense and a remarkable view of phone sex.

2) "Editor in Chief" by Cindy Patton, *Bad Attitude*, as published in *Fag Rag*, Summer 1984. I screamed in the middle of this one. A lesbianesque Firesign Theatre sketch: outrageous, satiric, and right on the clit.

3) "Tennessee" by Pat Suncircle, *On Our Backs*, Winter 1987. "I first met Rohn in the summer down South. The weather was hot and the air was close and heavy with dry grass and small dead animals. Snakes slid out of their skin." One of the most atmospheric and arousing pieces of erotica I have ever read.

4) "The Phoenix Chair" by Susan M., *On Our Backs*, Summer 1986. When I first received this story for consideration, I was shocked. I said, "I can't print this!" Of course, I realized that was the very reason I should. A pure and meticulous fire scene that will burn in memory.

5) "Ginny at Tea" by Minns, *On Our Backs*, Summer 1986. Minns is a fine and prolific erotic writer. Here she does what so many others have attempted miserably to create: a lesbian version of *Story of O*. Elegant, dreamlike.

6) "The Initiation" by Rebecca Ripley, *On Our Backs*, Spring 1987. Did you get palpitations watching Sigourney Weaver in "Alien"? So did Rebecca Ripley, who conceived the best butch on butch ever, in the setting of sci-fi military life.

7) "Girl Gang Bang" by Crystal Bailey, *Coming to Power*, edited by SAMOIS, Alyson Press, 1981. The first lesbian

fiction I ever successfully masturbated to. I pull this story out every year for a reunion.

8) "The Three" by Joan Nestle, *A Restricted Country*, Firebrand Books, 1987. Nestle wrote "Butch Fem Relationships: Sexual Courage in the 50s," for *Heresies* in 1981. Since then, she has been the queen of the butch/femme aesthetic. In this story, an older and younger femme travel with a young butch for an adventure on Fire Island. Nostalgic even for those who were never there.

9) "Olivia" by Barbara Ruth, *On Our Backs*, Fall 1984. Move over, Anne Rice. Olivia is a lesbian vampire who, while having no interest in leather herself, cruises a S/M support group for women on their period. In bed, Olivia convinces her date to take her menstrual sponge out, but the young woman is embarrassed: " 'Okay,' Bianca announced when she returned [from the bathroom]. 'It's out. There's liable to be a lot of blood. Don't say I didn't warn you.'

" 'I'll never say that. Whatever happens, I'll never say that.' Olivia stopped talking then."

10) "Phantom Nights" by Fanny Fatale, *On Our Backs*, Summer 1984. Remember those early lesbian feminist novels where the author tried doing away with masculine and feminine pronouns? Fanny Fatale proved to be the real revolutionary by designating "he's" and "she's" according to each character's erotic identity. " 'If I see one more butch tonight with his tie all loose and hanging off of him, I'm gonna go up and fix it good and tight!' Alexis voiced flatly." But by the end, Alexis is the one who gets her wagon fixed.

11) "Jessie" by Pat Califia, *Coming to Power*, edited by SAMOIS, Alyson Press, 1981. This early S/M piece spawned years of imitators, but none any better.

12) "A Short Story About a Penis" by Sarah Schulman, *On Our Backs*, Winter 1986. Okay, this isn't erotic, but it

is sexual fiction and it is the quintessential lesbian gender-fuck tale. Ann, the heroine, wakes up one morning with a penis attached where her clit used to be. She is nonplused. " 'I am a prick,' she says to herself."

Ann does manage to have some interesting experiences before she gets rid of her penis, including picking up a gay man in Central Park. "Ann had always wanted to say 'suck my cock' because it was one thing a lot of people said to her, and she had never said it to anyone."

When she comes in the comradely faggot's mouth, he tells her, " 'You taste just like my wife, when you come I mean, you don't come sperm, you know, you come women's cum, like pussy.'

" 'Oh, thank god.' Ann was relieved."

13) "The Succubus" by Jess Wells, *The Dress and the Sharda Stories*, Library B Productions, 1986. Mysterious, catholic, mother love. A leap from the ordinary, yuppie perversity.

14) "The Ditchdigger" by Tee Corrine, *Pleasures*, edited by Lonnie Barbach, Doubleday, 1986.

15) "Crybaby" by F., *On Our Backs*, Fall 1985. The only "dirty old lesbian" story I ever read:

"The door opens just a crack and all I can see is one of your little gleaming eyes.

"I whisper stupidly, 'It's me.' "

"You let me in and feel between my legs. You whisper, 'Where's your dick?'

"I push my reeking hand into your face. . . I let you grab my fingers between your pearly teeth.

" 'Bite harder,' I say. 'I don't have arthritis in that hand yet.' You bite harder and lick 'till there is almost nothing left to taste. I have my own teeth clenched like yours.

"I mutter, 'I'll tell you where's my dick. It's up my butt. I've had it held in place there with the cock ring for ages.' "

As I look over my Island 15, I see a list of great and crazy adventures. . . no ordinary life that I can compare my life to, no candle-lit dinners and walks on the beach. But I never fantasize about low-lit dinners and beach walks. I *could* conjure up having dinner eaten off of my breasts, and I would love to come across a sleeping beauty on the sand who opened her legs ever so slightly toward me. . .

Stay true to your own sexual imagination, and you'll not only be able to criticize lesbian erotica, you'll have a head start on writing your own.

VIVA LAS VEGAS

SPRING 1988

My dossier on the Secret Lesbian Porno Stars Network is fit to burst, after three days of Las Vegas conventioneering.

What? You say you've never heard of a Secret Lesbian Porn Stars Network? Perhaps it's because this association is *so* secret that most innocent convention-goers think they are attending the Adult Entertainment showroom of the Consumers Electronics Convention, a gadget and software show for retailers held biannually in Chicago and Las Vegas. Anyone who works at a Radio Shack or mom-and-pop video store can attend. Little do they know when they line up for some starlet's autograph that while said starlet may be marketing heterosexual voyeurism, her personal taste is quite another story.

Here's where the secret dyke porn stars come in.

I can see the headlines now: "Porn Biz: A Homosexual Front." Lesbians and die-hard bisexuals are most definitely in the front ranks of the adult movie business. In true Hollywood style, it's okay to publicly proclaim you

97

swing both ways, but it's Closet City when it comes to revealing one's preference for women. Although many actresses have confided to me that they are loyal readers of *On Our Backs*, there have been only two performers I know who came out of the closet: Debi Sundahl, *On Our Backs'* publisher, and Chris Cassidy, a former adult movie queen who went on to produce and star in her own lesbian-made video, *Erotic in Nature*.

It's assumed that the fans would all lay down and die if they knew that the biggest names in porn are queer. I rather think they'd be gladly educated and titillated. In an industry where everyone's so sexually liberated, there's a vicious double standard. The men I talk to from the video companies are almost in awe of all the actresses they perceive to be gay, but if any one of those women said, "Yes, I'm lesbian and proud," she would bear the burden of bringing the first blast of gay liberation to the ranks. Bubbles would be burst, crosses burned. In other words, it's the same old discrimination we face in every corner of the world, with just a special twist of hypocrisy.

This fear of "what the women are up to" blossomed at the recent trade fair, with the announcement of the formation of a new support group for female performers called the Pink Ladies Social Club.

The PLSC was started this winter in Los Angeles for women affiliated with adult films who want to provide frank support, education and assistance to each other, as well as work together on some special performance projects of their own. The PLSC is so new that it's hard to say what will happen, but the initial reaction from men in the business was pure macho hysteria. The big fear was oh-shit -they're-going-to-start-a-union, but since this is an all-female club, even that rumor was tempered by the paranoia that somehow this was a radical feminist conspiracy. One of the "Pinks" told me out of the side of her mouth that "for all I know we may just get together to fuck." What's a club without a social life?

The PLSC is a mixed group, but clearly it's a place for women to be comfortable about their bisexuality or lesbian preferences. This is a revolutionary idea in itself. Gay porn performers don't usually feel welcome into the bosom of the lesbian community.

The first time I ever heard gossip about a lesbian porn star was in 1980. Tigr, a former member of the gay clique I hung out with, was rumored to be making dirty movies, and what everyone wanted to know was, "Is it true she's sucking cock?—And does she like it?"

Such a rude question, I think, gets to the heart of lesbian fears and alienation from straight porn. The answer is, yes, they really do suck and fuck, and in answer to the second question, what does "like" have to do with it? Porn actresses are entirely underwhelmed by male nudity, male genitals, and male studliness in general. I find their attitude refreshing. Some women are proud of their screen skills at making a blow job look good, and some have a pleasant relationship with their male co-stars, while others don't have the time of day for the cocksmen once the camera stops.

In Tigr's case, after I heard the dish, of course I ran out to find a movie she was in, "A Thousand and One Erotic Nights." I immediately closed in on Tigr's scene with another woman. Her fingernails were short, smoothly manicured and unpolished. She went straight for this poor ingenue's G-spot, who just about flipped when she realized this was no ordinary straight fuck. If you want to spot the real dykes in the sex movies, watch their hands.

Lesbian strip shows, which emerged four years ago in San Francisco, are the most liberating settings I have ever

seen for women erotic performers. In case you haven't seen
the lesbian Burlezk video documentary, let me explain.
Every week for two years, and now sporadically, we've had
a lesbian erotica show in local gay bars, which feature
many professional dancers who work in the downtown sex
clubs. These women, who are so blasé in their "straight"
jobs, are as nervous as virgin brides when they perform
at Burlezk.

The very secret that most of them would normally rather
die than tell a group of dykes—"I'm a stripper"—sud-
denly makes them the hottest things on the lesbian dating
circuit. Rather than being viewed as confused or depraved,
the lesbian strippers earn a well-deserved reputation for
their guts, talent, and sexual sophistication.

When I came out in the seventies, the trend was that
anyone who truly cared for other women could be a lesbian.
You couldn't fuck *men*, of course, but you really didn't
have to fuck women either. You certainly didn't talk about
it if you did. As we entered the eighties, starved for erotic
recognition, the words on the gay welcome mat changed
to: "Lesbians are first and foremost sexual with one
another." And now, in recognizing lesbians in the sex business, the interpretation of sexual preference has more to
do with "preference" than with a lone sexual act. Women
who prefer women, yet who are sexually active with men
for money, for friendship, or for sport, are indeed kinky
compared to the rest of the gay or straight world, but
certainly identifiable as female sexual outlaws who walk
on the gay side.

What lofty thoughts! The real question is: What porn
star would I most like to be stranded on a desert island
with? Let's see, there's Sharon Mitchell, Erica Boyer, Juliet
Anderson, Georgina Spelvin, Seka, Angel Kelly, Porsche
Lynn, Cara Lott, Barbara Dare, Bionca. . . Oh, I can't

make up my mind. They're all such aggressive femmes, but the truth is, I like bulldaggers the best, who are in such short supply in the commercial porn world that for a moment in Las Vegas, I almost lost my mind and thought I was butch!

Such is life when two unfairly estranged worlds collide. Perhaps we'll start crashing into each other more often.

MACHINE CRAZY

SUMMER 1988

Is there such a thing as a sex nerd? I believe I qualify, at both high and low speeds. When I worked at Good Vibrations, one of the most interesting parts of the job was meeting the occasional inventor who walked in to demonstrate a new improved orgasm blender.

I was introduced in this way to the vibrator that hooked into your stereo system. The vibrator picked up the bass and basically hummed along with the music. Unfortunately, the vibrator was the usual battery-operated piece of junk that only mildly buzzed even if you were playing Run-DMC. Another great concept that never quite made it.

One fellow I met this way was Leonard Ginsberg, the creator of a little black box called the Humdinger. You plug this nugget into the wall outlet and then plug your electric vibrator into the box. When you turn on your toy, instead of the regular speed, you get a pulsing sensation— like a rapidly flipping light switch. The pulse makes it feel like the vibrator has a mind of its own, adding to your usual strokes a little unpredictability, and a lot more fun.

I collect dildos of every description. I made a discovery a couple years back when I received a brochure from Kansas City, advertising "the ultimate lifelike design, The Family Jewel." An accompanying photograph showed three different shades of meticulously detailed plastic penises. Good Vibrations ordered a sample, and I didn't expect much, despite the exuberant claims of the manufacturer.

But when I opened the shipment, I screamed bloody murder. I thought some nut had sent us a cadaver. This dildo is so realistic you could enter it in a science fair. The only unnatural thing about it, as male customers persistently pointed out, is that the "small" is gargantuan and the "large" is downright party size. But lesbians can be size queens without taking it personally, can't we, girls?

I dutifully brought a Jewel home to my lover to see what she had to say. She discovered that it fit perfectly between the third and fourth button of her Levis. (I knew that plastic scrotum was good for something!) It felt nice enough, firmer than the silicone dildos, but much more flexible than those hard plastic roto-rooters you see at the adult novelty shops.

There's one small problem: whether you decorate your partner with the Caucasian, the "mulatto" (that's Kansas City for you), or the black version, something about the coloring on the product doesn't mix well with a woman's vagina. We noticed after about a month's worth of sex play that our Family Jewel was looking like the Family Leper. When the color comes off, it looks nauseating. What to do? Other customers were complaining as well. The folks who make the Family Jewel assured us the pigment wasn't toxic, but my health wasn't the problem—I had an eyesore on my hands!

I've mentioned before that safe sex techniques are the best things to happen to my sex life since sliding down a pole, and my recent problem presented a case in point. I started using condoms on all my dildos so that I wouldn't constantly have to give them bubble baths, and I realized that the Family Jewel with a condom on was an unbeatable combination. My mulatto no longer mutates.

I can't leave safe sex alone without mentioning Stormy Leather's wonderful new invention, The Dammit, which they were inspired to create after reading of my lust for latex. The Dammit is a sort of harness/g-string, which holds a latex dam in place so that one's hands are free to make mischief elsewhere.

Last month I presented a safe sex talk at a women's erotica night in Santa Cruz as part of an AIDS fundraiser. I've done safe sex workshops in small groups and classes many times before. But when I stepped on stage that night with my black let's-play-doctor bag in front of four hundred people, I realized it was *showtime*. I threw mint and chocolate flavored dams into the audience. I invited them to suck my latex-gloved fingers. I told them every nasty thing I've ever done with a rubber barrier.

Finally, I asked for a volunteer to help model The Dammit. A slim grey-haired dyke climbed up to join me before the words were out of my mouth. Luckily, she was just the right size—the strap slid over her jeans like a custom fit.

"Spread your legs," I told her, before we had even exchanged names. After all, this was an exhibition.

". . . And this is how I would lick her," I called out to the crowd, and sank to floor, gracefully, I hope, my head ducking between her thighs. I pressed my face to her latex crotch, but there wasn't time to linger. After all, I couldn't leave her, a mere volunteer, facing this wild screaming mob. Santa Cruz was in hysterics, and I chalked it up to the sexual repression that this town's been suffering from since the sixties.

My act was over. Bidding all good night, I left the stage and walked right into a delirious group of backstagers.

"Do you know who that was you just went down on?" they asked.

"No. . . Why, is she a celebrity?"

"She's the campus Lutheran minister!" they shouted.

That's Santa Cruz for you—a feminist psychedelic college town that had them climbing the walls for Women's Erotica Night, and yet the only bookstore in town that carries gay literature won't sell *On Our Backs* because "it's violence against women."

Honest, my dental dams didn't hurt anybody, and they might save a few lives. The minister will vouch for me.

GAY DAY MAMA

FALL 1988

I have been going to the San Francisco Gay Parade for nine years, but always as a spectator, never a marcher. The idea of being stuck in some Lesbian Liberation in Our Lifetime contingent and thereby miss all the bands, costumes, Gay Fathers, Dyke Lawyers, and Androgynous Outrage was just too painful for me to contemplate. In 1987, I almost caved in and signed up for the Precision Whip Drill Team. But just watching the team march and snap by thousands of gaping spectators—who didn't know whether to laugh, scream or come in their pants—was a priceless vantage point I'll always treasure.

This year, a month before the Parade, my lover Honey Lee was gloating over her new BMW sport bike. "I'm going to join the Dykes on Bikes this year. Wanna ride?"

I fidgeted. I fussed. Dykes on Bikes leads the parade every year and tend to be the hottest looking women on the boulevard. On the other hand, who wants to be crawling along on a sport bike, a decoration on the back seat, while the rest of the excitement follows?

"Okay," I said. "I'll ride for the first few blocks, then I'm getting off to watch the others."

That morning Honey Lee went down to the junior high school where the Dykes on Bikes assemble. I took my time putting on every piece of leather I could find in our apartment. My prize was leather gauntlets and thigh-high leggings which, together with my cut-out cyclone tit minidress, made me look like Catwoman on the Rampage.

One of my favorite parts of Gay Day is getting there. Most city dwellers take public transit from their neighborhoods to the parade site. For example, at my streetcar stop, there were fifteen gay and delightful people waiting to pack into the train, which was already stuffed with happy homosexuals and one or two bewildered straights.

One of the reasons I get so exasperated with people who've never been to San Francisco Gay Day is they have never had the experience of *taking over a city* to celebrate. The whole world is turned upside down and the heterosexuals who would ordinarily be oppressing, ignoring and assuming god-knows-what about us are all of a sudden caught in our tidal wave. You can see on their faces what they're thinking: "Is there something wrong with me? Why aren't I gay? How come they're so happy?"

We're happy because that's what sexual liberation will do for you, buddy!

But back to the schoolyard. My ride was waiting for me at the end of the line, so I hopped on and checked my lipstick in the side mirror. Back Seat Decorations of the World Unite! I realized this was going to be a gas.

The second we hit the street, the crowd was roaring. I smiled at the audience on one side and they cheered. Cameras popped off by the dozen. Well, if they'd do that for a smile, I decided to try pointing my leather-braided legs in the air and pushing my cyclone tits to their limit.

What a reaction! I realized in a flash that inside every dyke on a bike there is a closet Rose Parade queen. The crowd treated each one of us like a returning war hero. I tried a little Princess Di wave. I tried humping my girlfriend from behind. Each gesture on my part drew another round of applause. I haven't had so much glory since I played Goldilocks in kindergarten.

When the bikes reach the end of their route, they park three deep in a one-block area. The serious cruising begins. Girls are running around with cameras and virtual index files of phone numbers. I left my lover for a few moments to strut my stuff. When I looked over to see how she was doing, a tall, silver-haired butch was leaning over to light her cigarette.

I don't think I've ever voyeurized a stranger coming on to my lover before. I got goose bumps.

All right, it was time to stop swishing and matchmaking and get over to the *On Our Backs* magazine booth, where we intended to sell two thousand copies of the new issue, plus a half dozen BORN TO FUCK buttons. I started over to our pink and black banner flapping in front of the City Hall fountain.

Leaving the buzz of Dykes on Bikes was a little like leaving an orgy—that post-performance letdown. I was just another queer in a sea of 260,000 others. But in mid-droop I noticed a group of feverish frolickers pointing and screaming in my direction. At ten yards away I couldn't recognize them, but obviously they were another squadron of fans—let me at 'em! We flew to each other like a Clairol hair spray commercial. The closer we got. . . the weirder it looked.

"She's a girl!" one of them gasped.

"They don't get any girlier," I replied.

I've been through this before. At over six feet in heels I

am frequently mis-identified at boys' bars and genderfuck gatherings. But to hell with their mistake. I *was* the perfect queen on Gay Day.

INVADERS FROM GIRL WORLD

JANUARY/FEBRUARY 1989

Maybe things have changed since Madonna started gracing New York City dyke bars, but I really wasn't prepared for the new avant garde lesbianism of the Big Apple. I was in town recently to promote my first book, *Herotica*, and I had my eyes opened. I have ridden the A train and I see the future.

My first glimpse of a new trend was at a party held at the latest lesbian slumming delight, a basement disco called Girl World that is installed under a slicker gay club, The World. As the night began, I was sort of an unlikely wallflower—wearing a short, strapless, red rubber minidress, but seated in the dark next to a table of my books. No one was buying.

One of my chaperones, Liz, grabbed me out of my doldrums. "You've got to meet my friend Jeep—I begged her to come here and meet you."

One look at Jeep and I could tell that she had to be begged to do anything—she was dressed in full leather topboy drag: jeans, studded jacket, motorcycle boots, Brando/cop hat.

I had seen Jeep once before, on television. She had appeared on the Phil Donahue Show about three months earlier wearing a completely different disguise. She was part of a panel with my idol, Betty Dodson, the female masturbation guru, discussing the joys of jerking off.

I had never seen a meaner Donahue audience in my entire life. Even though Jeep, Betty, and two others were dressed like squares and spoke politely about masturbation's benefits, this crowd would have treated an ax murderer with more sympathy. Besides tearing apart masturbation as the original fountain of evil, several in the studio particularly clawed into Jeep, who had to sit through accusations such as, "You must have to masturbate because you can't get a man." At that last comment, I got so riled I dialed Betty's number in New York. "I'm watching 'Apocalypse Now,'" I said, and she knew what I was viewing. "How can you be so dignified and brave in front of these cross-burners?"

"It's because I started having an out-of-body experience about halfway through the show," Betty said.

"Is that why you just smiled and said 'Yes, isn't it wonderful?' when one of the mob demanded to know if you were charging people to attend masturbation orgies?" I asked. Betty laughed.

"Say, who is that beautiful girl on the right—please tell me she's gay."

Betty confirmed my television mind reading and threw in a few gossipy details about Jeep that I couldn't possibly reprint here.

So here she was, the famous Jeep, at Girl World, looking like she could put tit clamps on the whole Donahue Show and leave them screaming for more. I introduced myself and said how much I admired her guts on national TV.

She put her hand on my sweaty latex thigh. "I want to

know everything about you."

What? Why does my mind go blank at lines like that? I waved my hand at the pile of *Heroticas* on the table. "This is my life," I said, sounding like Mother Theresa.

Jeep was not about to put up with my noble gestures.

"I have a present for you," she said, and pulled off her leather cap, reaching into the crown. She pulled out something blue and then slipped it into my palm. I clenched it and felt the foil edges. It was a Trojan. I uncurled my hand to verify that this was indeed the slickest cruising trick I'd ever seen in a lesbian bar—slip a girl a condom. Talk about saving lengthy explanations. I was impressed—and embarrassed.

Underneath my red latex exterior lay the finesse of an unreconstructed California hippie. I'm used to people offering back rubs, not condoms. Of course, now I know exactly what I *should* have said. I should have looked her straight in her green eyes and said, "Just how big is it?"

But Jeep was way ahead of me. "I have something else for you—a little performance," she announced.

Right here, right now? She stood up in front of me. The D.J. turned the record over. Jeep stepped back and held my eyes like we had a wire connecting our gaze. Then she began to strip. Oh, it was definitely a strip tease—she tossed her hat to one side and took her sweet time easing off her jacket. She had a harness on underneath. She was moving all slow and sexy, as if to say, "This is just for you, but I know that everyone is watching."

Everyone was. I'm so glad it was dark and smoky so that no one could see my face. I had just enough presence of mind to push away the few drunken clods who dared to cross our private stage.

Jeep didn't reveal anymore skin. She took my hand and pulled me to the center of the floor. The difference in our height must have overwhelmed her, but she didn't show it. I must be a foot taller, or, as my friend Sherry says, "You're so lucky, most girls are either level to your crotch or your tits."

I thought we danced real well together considering the spectacle. Heaven knows what she might have pulled out of her pocket next if I hadn't been interrupted by two old friends who pulled me out of the spell with a big bear hug.

"Jeep, it's too crazy with all the guests to pay as much attention to you as I want. Give me your number." I handed her a pen and the condom. She scribbled right inside the indented circle. Why can't these things be printed up like business cards?

The next night, I was being interviewed by an out-of-town lesbian journalist. She seemed ideologically supportive, but personally disappointed and unsatisfied by both *Herotica* and *On Our Backs*. At one point, she asked, "In your summer issue you have a story by Joan Nestle in which a woman asks to suck her woman lover's cock. How do you explain that?"

Oh dear, this was the feminist version of the "why-is-the-sky-blue?" question. I usually have a big reassuring rap to respond to this, but I was so tired this time. I picked up Jeep's condom from my hotel night stand.

"Why? Because some *lesbians* like to suck cock. That's really the most honest answer I can give you."

Things went downhill from there. When she was about to leave, I felt guilty for not giving her a better interview. "What do you really think?" I asked her. "Are you exasperated with *On Our Backs* and the whole lesbian sex media?"

"No, it's not that I don't appreciate your work—it's just that—well, when I want to get turned on, I don't read lesbian stuff anyway. I buy gay men's porn."

Click! Thank you, Lois Lane, for clearing up an hour-long misunderstanding. I should always remember this, on or off the Phil Donahue Show, in San Francisco or Manhattan—you can't tell a book by its cover.

GREAT BALLS FROM CHINA
AND OTHER TALL TOYS

MARCH/APRIL 1989

A few weeks ago a friend of mine told me she had persuaded a few of her more shy acquaintances to form a sex rap group. She explained these were the sort of women who were never going to visit a sex toy store no matter how congenial or woman-oriented it might be. Nonetheless, they were all curious about sex toys and Margaret asked me if she could borrow a few of my favorite items for show-and-tell.

"Sure, come over," I said, "But you have to bring them back by tomorrow. These are the foundations of my mental health."

"Is that all?" Margaret asked when she looked in my bag of tricks. She was disappointed that I only had a handful of items packed for her. But I wasn't about to get apologetic.

"Look, Maggie, we both know that the gadgets with the five rotating heads and automatic pilot don't hold a candle to a Magic Wand and a couple of nice-fitting dildos."

She understood my point and went off to make the best of it with her group, but our discussion got me to thinking. I've always wanted *more* from sex toys, but not in the direction most manufacturers were heading most of the time. The same men who make the ninety-three day programmable dual cam plaid-reversible whatchamacallits apply their same approach to inventing new sex toys, when what women are looking for is a substantial basic difference in style, comfort, power, and size.

Case in point: Joani Blank, owner of Good Vibrations, presented me with a prototype item from a man in the Midwest who sent along a desperately sincere four-page letter to describe all his hopes and dreams for his invention.

The contraption itself had one attachment for the clit, one for anus, one for opening to the vagina, one for inside the cunt, snaps to hook onto a garter belt, and a hand-held battery operated control set. All in the same piece of plastic.

Sure, I'd be a guinea pig. But my conclusions were predictable. Battery-operated anything doesn't do shit. And the little beast was ugly, with or without a snap-on lace garter belt. Not to mention that something with that many extensions and attachments is hardly going to fit every woman the same way.

If it's a vibrator, dammit, it should vibrate, not just buzz like a late night TV signal. I also prefer toys that are pleasing to look at, much like jewelry or any other adornment. Finally, you can never have too many sizes of something. Do we have to have Big and Tall sex toys to get the point across? Do we have to get Lane Bryant into the dildo business? There are not enough small things and there are not enough really big things. Same for fat and skinny.

All this reflection made me consider what has changed in the toy biz since I first started working in sex education. Our efforts have not entirely gone in vain. I remember in the old days when I was a buyer for Good Vibes. I used to plead, "Could you make these joy sticks in some other color than D.O.A. Caucasian?"

Seven years later, you can now walk into the tackiest adult store and find vibrators in magenta and aqua. Don't laugh, this is a direct response to the female voice in the sex market, so let's take the credit for it. We brought a little color and imagination to the world of genital plastic, a recognition of what these toys are for: pleasure, not guilt and secrecy.

The silicone dildos from Scorpio Products in New York revolutionized the dildo market in the early eighties. Gosnell Duncan, the inventor and producer, understood the importance of size, variety, and sensuality in his design. Now, six years after he began, we have the first two lesbian dildo producers, small and experimental, but with the desire to make a difference in a world that Doc Johnson (source of so many rubber "novelties and marital aids") has abandoned to mediocrity.

Trilby Boone, our first lesbian toy creator, says she was always concocting custom dildos to please her lovers. She would heat up one of the ugly orange rubber jobs over the gas range and then carve away at it with her pocket knife. Cindy Burns, the other talented entrepreneur, had less romantic beginnings but nevertheless saw an obvious need: everyone has been dissatisfied with the quality and availability of commercial sex toys.

I suppose you want to know what these new dildos look like. Trilby's models are like illustrations from an artist's sketchbook: dildos in the shape of dancers' legs, dolphins, corn on the cob, and goddess figures, to name a few. She has items as slim as a pinkie finger and, at their widest, about two inches around. There are a couple of models that look like something went wrong at the play-dough factory, but her best designs are adorable.

Cindy's collections, on the other hand, are not the least bit cute. They have a more primal, space fantasy look to them. They are bigger and weightier than anything else I've seen, and the styles are simple: either cock-like or subtly fluted molds. Honestly, the two women's personalities come out in their work. Cindy is the kind of dyke you would meet and say, "Take me away master, use me as you will"; whereas Trilby is the sort of gal to whom you would say, "Make it pretty for me honey—show me what you can do." Obviously, a girl needs both.

I'm so proud that women's creativity and good sense is finally expressing itself in businesses that we can all take advantage of. We've always been good at scavenging off the mainstream sexual entertainment world, making the factory models work for us, and discovering our own delights in the kitchen cupboard or the garden. But how often do women take the plunge and make their treasures accessible to others? This has been our weak point: going public.

One last tip for scavengers. The latest thrift shop for erotic invention is health food or Chinese medicine shops. I found out what was cooking last summer when a good friend presented me with a pair of Chinese Healing Balls; beautiful silver orbs, a little smaller than tennis balls, set in a red and black satin case. Inside the balls are weights that sound like distant chimes. Supposedly you do figure eights with these balls in your palms to relieve arthritis, high blood pressure, and other ailments.

Well, I had a different health plan in mind. These fat pearls looked like what ben wa balls were suppose to be but never lived up to. I inserted one in my cunt, and smooth and round as it was, it slid in easily. At first I felt a little like Mother Hen. I wanted to sit on someone's lap and play golden goose. I stroked my clit for a while and felt the ball rolling gently inside me. . . I just had to try to insert the second one.

These balls didn't feel quite like fisting because each one of them is smaller than any adult's hand, but the two together require a nice bit of room. I was very wet, and I could hardly stay serious enough to complete my experiment, but I edged the second globe past my lips. It wouldn't quite go in. The base fluted out at my cunt's opening. Heaven. Almost in/almost out is my preferred method of going insane.

I rocked on my quilt and the chimes echoed from my belly. I felt like a Tibetan sex chant. I climaxed and the first silver egg tumbled out. The second ball stayed hugged in the upper walls of my vagina until my vagina relaxed about fifteen minutes later. I never noticed how long it takes for my vagina to return to its indilated state, so this was an unexpected scientific bonus.

Do I have Richard Nixon to thank for my introduction to the Chinese material world? Apparently these balls are just one of the many stimulating products one can find in the new market opened up by America's interest in acupuncture and traditional healing. How will lesbians take the lead in the new oriental eroticism? I think I'll go chant some more and think about it.

THE MORE THINGS
CHANGE. . .

MAY/JUNE 1989

I made my yearly pilgrimage to Hollywood to attend the Porn Oscars this spring, and I had the extra stimulation of making an appearance for my anthology, *Herotica*, at A Different Light Bookstore in the heart of gay Los Angeles.

There I was speaking to an SRO crowd that was so warm my glasses were fogging up, and right in the front row was carrot-top Cherelle, the first dyke I ever went to bed with. When I turned a few shades of red, I assumed the audience just thought I was getting overheated about erotic censorship.

But Cherelle wasn't the only one making me blush with nostalgia. I went to high school in West L.A., which during the mid-seventies was a beehive of teenage lesbian feminists, hippie bisexuals and proto-punk anarchists. In 1974, I would have thought you had a screw loose if you weren't politically and sexually committed to women. However, as I have reminisced several times, my lesbian politics were a lot hotter than my lesbian sexuality, and when Cherelle first met me, I was no Susie Sexpert. I don't know how she can read *On Our Backs* with a straight face when she remembers perfectly well that I lay stiff as a board in her bed and, afterwards, couldn't say a word to her for months.

I had sex with, and initiated, many girls before Cherelle, but with a great deal less anxiety. They weren't gay, they weren't from the bar crowd, and, although I didn't know the word at the time, they weren't butch.

The first time a woman ever described herself as butch to me was the time I finally insinuated myself into the beach flat of my high school heroine, Barbara Jean. BJ was the first person in our high school to wear a DYKE button and she turned every assignment in our American Lit class into a gay liberation exercise. She passed me notes written in a leaky blue fountain pen, bits of Sapphic homage to the female body and stinging hilarious (okay, tenth-grade hilarious) criticism of male chauvinism. She also looked like a SoCal tomboy goddess—blonde, tanned, muscular, with eyes that matched her lavender slogans.

She didn't reciprocate my infatuation; it was a miracle that I ever ended up between her sandy sheets. I remember reaching between her legs to touch the hair that looked as soft as it did on her head, and she pushed me away with a start, biting me hard on the shoulder.

"Now you know—I'm butch." I didn't get it. Did that mean I couldn't make love to her? Did it mean she had a vicious little mouth? I was working up the nerve to ask her when someone knocked on the door.

"Ssssh," Barbara Jean said. "It might be Sherry." That was her ex.

"Well, why don't you open the door?" I asked. BJ hissed

again and jumped out of bed, running into the bathroom and locking the door behind her. The knocking continued. I remember she had The Spinners' "For the Love of You" playing over and over. I must have listened to it fifteen times before Sherry gave up knocking and yelling and split. I left with BJ still holed up in the john. *This* was butch?

I headed back to my more familiar territory of androgyny and feminism. You know, it really wasn't all that square at the time. I remember a whole gang of us going to see a major women's music concert: Holly Near, Cris Williamson, and Meg Christian. We were so keyed up afterwards that a dozen of us proceeded over to some lucky girl's house (parents gone for the weekend), ate psilocybin mushrooms, and cranked up "The Changer and the Changed" on the stereo. Before you could say "filling up and spilling over," everyone was making out. A women's music orgy! This particular ranch home was equipped with every type of consumable fare. I raided the refrigerator and covered my best friend at the time, Linda, with strawberry, avocado and salami slices from head to toe and ate them off of her.

Sisterhood was indeed powerful, and also enhanced by the psychedelic period we were in. They always told you drugs lower your inhibitions, and I will be forever grateful for those early consciousness-expanding experiences.

My first lesbian lover was Monique, who was French and a year younger than I, though much more worldly. One day she decided to teach me how to kiss properly with the assistance of some peyote buttons.

Monique was the first real sensualist I was ever intimate with. She brought a bowl of roses to her bed and told me to inhale the fragrance before I ate the buttons. She had the Stones' "Sticky Fingers" on her tape player, and outside there was a terrific windstorm shaking the eucalyptus grove that surrounded the shed she lived in. When we started to get high, she took me into the shower and soaped me all over like she was bathing Aphrodite. Yes, I was ready to learn all about kissing. She kissed me for hours and held my hands above my head so I couldn't do anything else. She told me never to push my tongue down someone's throat again, and I learned my lesson.

This little period of sexual instruction was, if you can't guess, utterly without sexual aids of any kind. I learned to use my mouth and was only literate with my hands outside a woman's body. I strongly believed in the Myth of the Vaginal Orgasm, and my early experiences with fucking just seemed to confirm the feminist politics of the day. If I had been introduced to a dildo at that time, I would have thought it was evidence of the most pathetic self-esteem. I didn't value masculinity in men; why would I want it in a woman?

Of course, I was attracted to masculinity even at that time, but it was labeled under more Amazonian descriptions: strength, tenacity, militancy. I saw these qualities in myself too, which made me even more confused. The things an unhatched femme has to go through!

Nowadays, I occasionally have a date with another toy box queen, but I still find that my first time in bed with a lover is a display of how well we learned the basics: your mouth, my hands. Kissing the way she likes it. Getting fucked the way I learned to love it. At first I thought I was simply scared to say on a first date, "Baby, strap on that Family Jewel, why don't you?" because it would reveal my fantasies a little too starkly. I certainly see that same apprehension in the woman who wants to "do something" to me but either isn't aware of the equipment or is shy, like I can be, to admit that desire.

Other times, though, it's not sublimated wishes that keep us bare-handed and unadorned. It's just that plain old naked still feels good; it's not a hippie cliché or a feminist directive. In my case, it reminds me of a time I wouldn't have missed for all the dildos in Dykeland.

OVER THE DAM

JULY/AUGUST 1989

I'm a spontaneous public speaker. I may not have stood on a soapbox yet, but I've delivered a call to arms from a milk crate. Controversy just adds to my stage hots. Nothing warms me up like a high school sex education class where the first student asks, "Why are lesbians so fat and ugly?" And on those special occasions, when an elite event can be delightfully disrupted by a single clear voice, I'm in SRO heaven. I mean, I didn't plan to get up in the War Memorial Opera House and ask Susan Sontag what exactly she thought of lesbian-made porn, but I'm so glad I did. The look of disbelief on her face was worth the thousand words she didn't say.

Consequently, when the San Francisco AIDS Foundation asked me to speak on a women's AIDS panel, I didn't hesitate—at first. As the coordinator, Marsha, explained how the panel would be made up of experts on medical, legal and family issues relating to women's concerns, I interrupted her with a start.

"Do you mean that the audience I'll be speaking to is women *with* AIDS?"

129

"Well, either that, or their partners, or simply seropositive women who may or may not be symptomatic," she explained.

My head swam. My mouth mumbled through the date and time with her. I suppose I sounded ideal when I told her that this was the kind of safe sex education I'd wanted to do for ages. I told her I didn't want to be Ms. Condom anymore, that I was ready for the nitty-gritty.

But, truthfully, I was scared shitless of the nitty-gritty. I have been raving for years that women, and in particular lesbians, have to own up to AIDS' effect on our lives. But now I was going to speak to a whole room of women living with AIDS, and I felt like I had a date with the devil and the deep blue sea.

Women with AIDS face isolation, invisibility and outright ostracism; they live with the worst kind of vulnerability. To meet these women, en masse, was to go into the lions' den, as far as I was concerned. Here I thought I'd finally wiped out my own AIDS-phobia, and then it grabbed me by the neck.

Even beyond dealing with my own trepidation, I knew this event would shake me up. There is virtually no information or resources for women with AIDS, and *that* is both sickening and scary.

There were about a hundred people gathered in the lecture hall. As I found out during our discussion, about half were AIDS caregivers, and the others were HIV-positive women and their lovers. A significant group of lesbians attended. But the part that got me, the stupid obvious thing I didn't expect, was that most of the affected women were so young. I met a couple of middle-aged seropositive women, but the rest were in their twenties. The caregivers in the crowd were the ones who looked like they needed nutrition and exercise. It was the HIV-positive women who sparkled, the kind of girls you would notice walking down the street.

Of course, this was an unusual group; these were the women who had taken the most activist, pressing role in their diagnosis and treatment. I met the women who knew that a panel like this existed, and they were certainly in the minority.

I began my talk by explaining I could learn much more from them than they could from me. Since the mainstream has offered no information about HIV-positive women's sexuality, we could only start at the ground floor and share each other's experience. I wasn't about to give a condom-on-a-banana talk to a group of people who were dealing with the idea that their very bodies could be poisonous. The crucial identity point for women with AIDS, like all women, is that they were raised to be fearful and ignorant of sexual desire, to be estranged from their bodies. To then be infected with the stigma of AIDS must feel like the ultimate denial of anything good, enriching and *female* about sexual experience.

A woman struggling with AIDS-phobia and her own positive diagnosis is confronted with the dilemma of loving and healing her sexuality in a way she has likely never prepared for before. Of course, many women won't deal with it, ever. They will become celibate, unsexual, antierotic.

I asked the audience to jot down on a slip of paper some quick thoughts on a series of questions.

Since their HIV-positive diagnosis, did these women:

1) have more or less sex with a partner;

2) masturbate more or less;

3) give up some sexual practice they really loved, and, if so, what was it?

4) discover any *new* sexual practice they loved, and, if so, what was that?

I asked the partners of the infected women to answer for themselves, and I asked the remaining non-infected women to answer the questions as if they were seropositive and had to make such decisions.

I madly counted up the replies during the rest of the panel. The biggest surprise was the difference between the people who "had it" and the people who didn't. I would say the non-infected respondents were more pessimistic—they seemed to think that if they were diagnosed positive tomorrow, they'd just crawl into a casket and wait to be carted away.

The majority of HIV-positive women, in every case, said they had less sex with a partner since their diagnosis. But 32% of the HIV-positive women said they had either the same or more sexual relations with their lovers, which I think is a sizable minority. These women were staying close to their sexual lives.

Fifty-seven percent also said they masturbated as much or more than usual, but in this case, it was the large minority—the 43% who reported masturbating *less*—that made me sad. There is zero risk in making love to oneself, and yet when sexual self-esteem goes out the window, masturbation seems to be one of the most potent experiences that gets cut.

Seventy-nine percent of the HIV-positive women, and 90% of their partners, said they had given up something very important to them: unprotected oral sex. I have *never* seen a group of people get this hot under the collar about cunnilingus.

After all these years of the dildo wars, pitting one dyke against the next as to whether she liked to get fucked or not, it was refreshing to hear people demanding the pleasure of oral sex for its own fabulous merits, not because it is "egalitarian," or politically correct. I will never eat pussy the same way again!

But check it out. Fifty percent of the audience said they had incorporated *new* sexual behavior that they would never want to give up. The most commonly listed were vibrators and fantasy scenes.

The big difference here between infected versus non-infected responses was that the people who were not seropositive imagined that they would turn to more gentle, sensuous foreplay activities if they were practicing exclusive safe sex. The seropositive group, however, immediately understood the orgasmic intent of my question and told me what they needed and wanted to *get off*.

Two HIV-positive women did say they now enjoyed "gentleness" and "more sensitive communication," but I could tell by the rest of their list that they were lovers with men. One straight woman said how she now loved getting finger fucked, and all I could think of was, "You had to wait for this?!"

Something puzzled me about the furor over oral sex. The women who spoke up about it seemed convinced that mouth-to-pussy contact was no risk if the woman wasn't bleeding or suffering any cuts, sores, or blisters. Certainly the absence of blood or semen would make a powerful argument for no-holds-barred cunnilingus.

I asked them, "If you're not worried about oral sex, why have so many of you given it up?"

One woman burst out, "Because if you tell anyone you're HIV-positive, they don't want to *touch* your pussy, let alone eat it!"

That about sums it up. We can talk about safe sex techniques from dusk until dawn, but it's a lot of precise talk about plastic and positions. The real dilemma of women's sexuality and AIDS is fear, stigma, humiliation, and estrangement. The goal is to feel close, sexy and passionate—and turn on and dig yourself.

The techniques of safer sex can distract us from the bare bones. For example, one girl asked me, "I was with a lover for six years who had AIDS. I've been alone for a year since and I'm just about ready to go out again so I want to know how to use rubber dams."

That was the moment I was waiting for. I handed her a couple of mint flavored squares and said, "I can tell you how to use a barrier in two minutes, but it seems like that's the least of your dilemma. How do you feel about having sex again? Do you fantasize about oral sex, do you long for it, are you afraid of it?"

These questions could be applied to any woman. In this forum, with these women, the basic sexual choices were simply illuminated by the fact that it was now a matter of life and death.

Someone handed an anonymous note up to the panel: "What is known about lesbians with AIDS and lesbian safe sex practices?"

There were perfectly competent health care people on the panel to answer the question, but I wasn't about to sit through another just-the-facts-ma'am recital.

"The story with lesbians and AIDS," I said, "isn't about the three cases of woman-to-woman transmission reported in medical journals. The story is sitting here in this room. We all know that the medical establishment has ignored lesbian sexuality in regard to AIDS, but the one group of people you think would give a shit—other lesbians—are just as guilty of denial as the Centers for Disease Control.

"The main way lesbians get infected is through men and IV drug use. Since most human beings, and that *does* include lesbians, are neither exclusively homo or heterosexual, it's not surprising that many lesbians, who would never think of themselves as bisexual, are touched by this epidemic. But the lesbian public front is this pure-

as-the-driven-snow bullshit which keeps women from being
honest and unafraid with one another. We have now
reached a point, because of AIDS, where we either confront
our taboos and get real, or we're going to watch our own
silence and secrecy kill us.

"I'm not afraid of male contamination, of losing the
lesbian essence. I'm afraid of lesbians losing our empathy
for each other because we've let our fears and prohibitions
about sex tear us apart."

One of the dykes came up to me afterward and said, "I
go to the twelve-step programs, you know, and I tell them
my status, and the other lesbians can't look me in the eye.
I'm butch (she didn't have to tell me), which makes them
even more confused. . . Of course I fucked men: for drugs,
for money, for the hell of it. But I know who I am."

"So how do you deal with them?"

"I don't. If they can't handle me, I don't need their shit.
It's a shame, though."

I couldn't blame her for not trying to raise their consciousness all at once. This is exactly what I meant by
isolation. By comparison, the other HIV-positive lesbians
who hung out after the panel were obviously very tight,
enjoying the kind of closeness I used to see at gay bars in
out of the way places.

At the end of my presentation, a few people thanked me
for showing off my sex toys. One woman said, "I like that
you said the vibrator was *yours*, and didn't just tell us,
'It has been known to be effective. . .'"

"God, yes, all these toys and books are my own." I
brought them not because I thought they would be so new,
but because I wanted to demonstrate how making the first
change in sexual behavior is the hardest. The next changes
come much more sweetly. I started with a vibrator, but
then that opened me up to so much more—not just things

to buy and consume, but an understanding of my capacity, a hook into my imagination. My sexuality developed more in the past seven years than in all the twenty-three preceding.

There was so much more to say. We got fifteen minutes on a panel to talk about sex and we needed a good fifteen hours. Yet it was the most powerful fifteen-minute sexual discussion I've ever been a part of. I'm ready for the nitty-gritty now. I'm taking off the gloves.

(Don't worry, I've got plenty more under the bed.)

A STAR IS PORN

SEPTEMBER/OCTOBER 1989

A re you ready for the gay nineties—or is it the *post-gay* nineties? Sexual liberation is going to have a new theme in the next decade and the motto is: "Get Over Yourself."

Five years ago I was entreating readers of the first issue of *On Our Backs* to discover that "penetration is only as heterosexual as kissing." Now the dildo wars are over and guess what? We won. So stick it in and enjoy it. Lesbian sex is still a blank look in many parts of America's closet, but the trend—the fashion, if you will—is lesbians on parade. Even straight couples are buying dildos now, and only their lubricant knows who's playing the boy and who's playing the girl.

When I came out in the women's movement of the seventies, I know I was part of an unprecedented generation of novice dykettes. But what's going on with young women today makes my crowd look puny. I don't know quite how they're figuring it all out without the benefit of herb teas and consciousness-raising groups, but I see more queer young things running around today than I did ten years ago.

They're sporting crew cuts together with frosted lipstick, suspenders with high heels, a gay style with pop culture. And this time the gay flair isn't being single-handedly developed by the boys. It's the women who have the most handsome feathers.

Please don't tell me that's androgyny—I have a faded flannel shirt to remind me of what that turned out to be a euphemism for. It wasn't the best of masculinity and femininity *en flagrante*—it was zero femininity and milk toast butch.

That's why now, when we want to complement someone's visual menu, we say "genderfuck" instead of androgynous.

Words have changed a lot. In the sixties it was "orgies," in the seventies, "group sex," and now it's a word right out of Pee-Wee Herman's vocabulary: "Play Parties." Play party emphasizes a social occasion, not a bacchanalia, a game atmosphere rather than psychoanalysis.

Play parties are for the pleasure and reputation of only a few, though. By far the most popular trend is kinky monogamy and erotic merchandising. The only question I had when I was invited to my first Jill-Off party was: "Where are the outlets?"

I see outlets in your future, girlfriend. I see two hundred and fifty volts conversing though your swollen cunt lips, and I see a strap-on looming straight ahead.

Hand-held dildos are out, strap-ons are in. You need your hands for other things, like holding her arms over her head so you can whisper your nastiest phone sex script into her ear.

If your lavender life-like dick slips out, for goodness' sake, do us a favor and guide it back in without a lot of flailing around. Or just lay still and make her do it—she's probably in the biggest hurry.

Bigger *is* better; I will predict this without blushing. With strap-ons you need a couple of inches extra just to play with and stay connected. If you are one of those girls who is still saying, "No, no, no, it's too big!" you're either turning me on, or you're the last person in Cincinnati who won't use a good lubricant. Slippery does it.

I mentioned talking dirty before, and that's definitely *in*—we'll be talking more and *wearing* more in bed. Anyone who is still crawling in between the sheets buck naked is a total bore. We are off the farm now, Gidget: there's no turning back.

Susie Sexpert predicts that S/M will continue setting vogues for the latest trends in plain old passionate love-making. Pierced labia, uncomplicated bondage, spanking, sucking toes, vibrator torture and begging for it are all just business as usual. Please don't even consider yourself an S/M dyke unless you have at least four whips and a set of monogrammed alligator clips.

We're going to start talking about what we do instead of who we supposedly are. Don't say "I'm an S/M lesbian," when you could be saying, "I fantasize eating out my manicurist on the bathroom floor with her mouth gagged by a rubber ball." Or, "I pinch my nipples when I masturbate until they're hard as points." And, "Fist me until the sweat drips off my lip." Isn't that much more enlightening?

Every lesbian video and best-selling book you'll see in the near future is going to address lesbian sexuality. The whole Amazon nation is going to get their two bits in. You won't be heard any longer for simple criticism—it's either put up or shut up time in the lesbian media circus. We don't want to hear any more angst without alternatives. Sex theory is welcome; neuroses masquerading as analysis are not.

Lesbians are the vanguard of cross-pornographic pollination these days. We've been the first to go public with how fun it is to check out how the other half, third, and quarter swings. We've been as thoughtful about porn as we have been stimulated by it, and now that analysis is going to come in handy. Lesbians will make porn respectable. I mean it.

The best thing about the anti-porn movement among lesbians was that at least we got a chance to be intellectual about it, unlike the traditional bible-thumping put-downs.

Following the same process, if you can exercise your brain thinking about how and why sexual images affect you so strongly, you're well on your way to joining the Erotic Literacy Society. Sexuality is the artist's domain in the next decade. We're going to do it all night and write it, paint it, and video tape it all day.

Okay, AIDS. I'd love to have the winning number on this one. AIDS is one of the vicious incentives toward nineties sexual diversity. It will leave a lasting consciousness and preventative behavior towards all STDs.

People will be thinking about safer sex techniques on a sophisticated and personal basis. Gloves and condoms are here to stay. Microwave Saran Wrap will be the barrier of choice for those who avoid oral-genital contact, and you can use any extra rolls for a nice mummification scene. Bleeding gums are probably the biggest danger in cunnilingus, not pussy juice. I predict more brushing and flossing.

Personal sex ads are in. Fisting on the first date is in. Switching is in. Teasing (her cunt, not your hair) is very in. And then giving her exactly what she wants is in. Pleasing yourself is going to be more of a pleasure. I can't wait for the nineties. Do the Right Thing.

ABSOLUTELY PIERCED

NOVEMBER/DECEMBER 1989

"Why'd ya do it?"

Some people hear that question their whole lives, but it's only been popped to me since I got my labia pierced.

No matter what impression you've gathered in these columns, I have always been an obedient, people-pleasing kind of girl: I never fantasized running away to the circus; I wouldn't consider wearing, having, or branding a mohawk. I do have one faded tattoo but it only covers a small patch on my shoulder blade—a fountain pen with roses laid over a sword.

So what's with putting a ring through one nether lip? I got the idea four years ago when my friend Fanny decided to pierce her labia and we all agreed to photograph the event for *On Our Backs*. I remember two things from that afternoon—Fanny was cool as a cucumber from start to finish, sporting a perfect gold ring that shone through her blonde pubes at the end of our session. Her piercer, Raelyn Gallina, was one of the most down-to-earth body-reverent women I'd ever met. I'm surprised she doesn't have a line around the block of petitioners seeking just a touch from her healing hands.

I replayed that afternoon many times over since 1985. I watched Fanny strip at the Mitchell Brothers burlesque theater, removing gaudy baubles from her ear and swinging them, like an exotic pendulum, from her pussy. I'll never forget the time one man in the audience literally keeled over in his plush seat, gasping, "I'm going to fucking die," as she swayed and dipped inches from his awe-struck view. It was pretty exciting.

I met other men and women who pierced their genitals, and in each case, no matter what I thought of their body parts, I found the jewels made them appreciably more beautiful. I also found it—you can dim the lights now—irresistibly romantic. No firelight or white lace hankies for me—just a labia ring and thou art mine. So much more serious than a sweater pin, a thousand times more erotic than a wedding band. It's an emblem of sexual possession and empowerment all in the same tiny circle of stainless steel.

Or, as my friend Dominga said when I pulled down my pants for show-and-tell, "How good to put something so beautiful in the most beautiful part of your body." *Exactemente*.

If you're like most of my friends, you've raced through all my tender descriptions to get to what outsiders perceive to be the heart of the matter: "Didn't it hurt?"

Well, we took a picture. There is my dead-honest needle-point reaction, and it lasted two seconds, tops. There was a tiny amount of blood and I saved the stained Kleenex for posterity.

I was apprehensive about the pain all those years I fantasized about doing it. The key to my courage was when I realized that, while I'm a full-blown sissy where my own body is concerned, I have the nerves of a tiger when it comes to protecting my friends and family. When my sister-in-sex-work, Lisa LaBia, arrived in town from Minneapolis, we decided that the family that pierces together stays together.

I was so full of myself being brave for her—squeezing her palm reassuringly—that you could have knocked me over with a feather when she shook loose my hand and said, "I want to go first." I watched her big blue eyes get wide as pies as Raelynn pushed the needle through, and she threw her head back in the prettiest little cry of anguish I ever saw.

I'm afraid I wasn't nearly as sexy at the crucial moment. My split-second reaction was one of pure anger, and the thought that crossed my brow was, "Who the hell let you in?"

But afterwards you could not get the mirror out of my hands. I love the amethyst bead that lies so contentedly on my right lip. It healed completely in three days with just a little Neosporin to help ease the initial tenderness.

No, it does not get in the way of fucking. It's right in the middle of my labia, neither touching my clit nor my urethra. I don't feel it unless someone touches it. I did discover a surprising sound effect the first time I used my vibrator. Not as pure a tone as a tuning fork, but I'll pass on sound for the superior sensations.

I'm not the type to attribute unexplainable spiritual forces to the daily events of my life. But my piercing certainly provoked rushes of irrational feeling that I couldn't have predicted beforehand.

Compared to the first day of my period, when I was fourteen and bored to death with the whole thing, my piercing had me in an ecstatic female fever. It was all I could to do to keep from yelling "I am WOMAN, hear me roar!" I'm convinced now that Helen Reddy must have multiple genital piercings.

I spend a great deal of time assuring folks that the pain of piercing is fleeting compared to going to the dentist or stubbing your toe.

But, because this particular pain is premeditated and chosen, there *is* a pride and sweetness to it that I value as much in memory as I do the present adornment. If Jane Fonda can tell you to "feel the burn," why can't I? The pain was a sensational climax to a rite of passage I've felt traces of when I've aroused a lover to total madness or brought my own orgasm to the tips of my fingers.

Pussy Power: The clit that rocks the needle rules the world.

FAMOUS LESBIAN DILEMMAS

JANUARY/FEBRUARY 1990

Name a lesbian celebrity. Now name two lesbian celebrities. Getting stuck? Is the proud pronouncement getting trapped in your throat? When it comes to famous lesbians there are probably more exceptions, extenuating circumstances and clouded confidences than last year's entire edition of the *National Enquirer*.

The problem is that unlike gay men in every field of business and entertainment, lesbians are just as much in the closet today as they were in the old 1964 lesbian exposé novel, *The Grapevine*. One of my favorite chapters admits, "Some of the most beautiful and seductive stars in Hollywood are lesbians, but their public will never know."

I used to think that famous lesbians and bisexuals were concerned with the straight public destroying their careers if their secret was known. But from personal experience, I now wonder if such celebrities are more selfishly worried that other *lesbians* will ruin their social lives if they subject themselves to the gay community's critique. The gay public reveres rumored-to-be homosexual stars, but subjects ordinary out dykes to blistering reviews.

I've had my brush with lesbian fame. Darling, it's so lonely at the top! On stage, or signing autographs, I attract the most fascinating cluster of women touching my arm, whispering intimate secrets in my ear, exposing homemade dildos for my appraisal. But after the lights go down, and the chairs are folded up, I'm sitting by my lonesome in the auditorium, wondering what reproach will appear in the gay press the next day.

Sometimes one gutsy gal sticks around to offer me a bar tour, a joint, or an unpublished manuscript. She's shy but tenacious. She's not exactly my type, but I'm dying to be flattered. I'm Susie Sexpert! I'm supposed to be having insane sweat-soaked erotic adventures every night. What am I waiting for?

And there it is: the worst case of performance anxiety ever to hit the Richter Scale. This is why famous lesbians won't come out of the closet—celebrity bed death. Because Susie Sexpert might be the most electrifying lover on earth, and Jodie Foster might be the answer to all your romantic dreams, but Susie Bright could well turn out to be a crashing bore, and Jodie whatever-her-real-name-is, an insufferable little pill.

Yeah, say it ain't so. But sometimes I feel deliberately ornery in the face of high lesbian expectations. Fisting? Oh, I wouldn't dream of it. How can you respect me in the morning if we use silicone on the first date? No, you can't touch my Barbie Doll bondage collection! Is this what Martina goes through?

My sub-cult celebrity ego has been put in check, however. I have been taught a very important lesson. I have been put in my place by the most important lesbian nation heartthrob since Marlene Dietrich: country music star k.d. lang.

I don't own a k.d. lang album. My hairdresser, Miss
Rupa, turned me on to her. She was cutting me a set of
bangs, in her studio, when I interrupted, "What are we
listening to?" The record sounded like Patsy Cline and
Elvis singing in one single, buttery voice.

Rupa stared at me like I'd just been born. "k.d. lang is
playing this weekend at Caesar's Tahoe and you'd better
come to see her if you want to know the meaning of *alive*."

Well, why not? Rupa arranged for a group of us to take
a gamblers' bus from San Francisco to Tahoe, so we could
drink screwdrivers in style on the way there and supposedly
sleep on the way back—a twelve-hour junket. I could tell
Greyhound about the meaning of half-dead, but that's
another story.

The important part was, what were we going to wear?
Rupa is a smartly-styled girl and I didn't want to be embarrassed. I suggested I might wear my red latex strapless,
but Rupa advised against it.

"Look, we're going to be on a bus for five hours. You've
got to be comfortable. I'm going casual all the way." She
was right.

Friday, one in the afternoon, Greyhound bus terminal.
In walks Rupa with a foot-high cotton candy pink bouffant
hairdo, black bustier, black crinoline, lime green stretch
pants, leopard skin knee highs, plaid Thai silk heels and
a white leather motorcycle jacket.

You casual bitch! I would have slapped her but she was
just too perfect. "Don't worry," she apologized, "I'll do
you on the bus."

What were we going to *do* to me on the bus? Strap on a
seat cover? But to her credit, Rupa set me and every gam-
ble-holic in that bus on their ear. With one can of hair
spray and a tiny purse brush, she teased my hair into a
mile high castle. My make-up was Ann-Margret. A black

bra pulled from Miss Rupa's port-a-bar replaced my T-shirt and the effect was complete. We looked like the night Billie Jo McAllister jumped off the Tallahassee Bridge.

The bus was late for the show. We ran into the lounge and took our seats in the middle of k.d.'s "Cryin'." I thought, this canary really does give me goose bumps. Some straight couple on our left were arguing: "She's certainly not very feminine"—"But you can't touch that voice."

Well, I think she's feminine—a little tomboy femme with lots of mischief. She doesn't make any admissions to her adoring girl fans, but she certainly teases us to death.

It was encore time when Rupa grabbed my arm. "We've got to get down in front so she can see us!"

I flinched but followed. I suspected some casino security beef would probably put his hands on my 'do. But Rupa propelled us to the edge of the stage just as k.d. opened her pipes for the one last time.

She stopped. She stared at us. "Look at these lovely bouffants . . . could we get a spotlight over here on these girls?"

Rupa didn't hesitate. She reached for k.d.'s arm and stepped onto center stage, pulling me up with her. The lights twinkled against k.d.'s blue sequin jacket. She turned to the crowd and said, "You know what they say in Nashville—the higher the hair, the closer to God."

I looked into k.d.'s eyes, and tilted my head towards Rupa. "She loves you so much." I don't know if that comment was miked or not. I took Rupa's hand and led her off-stage. We were applauded mightily.

A few high notes later, the show was over and Rupa and I were surrounded by "Lang Thangs." They screamed and screamed. Remember those Beatlemania movies? Like that. Hyperventilating and squealing and touching us 'cause we'd touched her.

"This is the most exciting moment of my entire life," said one girl who vicariously drank up our moment of glory like cat's milk. After hearing that, I started to feel more like a wig and less like a person. Why, if I only had a copy of *On Our Backs* to flag on stage when the spotlight came my way! If only I was a mysterious talent who never said a word about her private life but fulfilled every dewy-eyed homosexual crush!

Oh, k.d., I wish you'd tell me what the price of privacy is. Maybe I could tell you a thing or two as well. Maybe you'd just like to know who did our hair. Give me a call.

WHAT TO EXPECT

MARCH/APRIL 1990

I'm expecting. My very own bundle of joy is due in a blaze of Gemini glory on June twelfth. My first child is on its way.

Lest you fear this kink-filled column is going to degenerate into a pediatric podium, let me assure you that one of my first concerns as Susie Sexpert is to uncover the secrets of prenatal sex, particularly prenatal lesbian sex. What I've learned so far is a scandal.

In a nutshell, the information available to the pregnant lesbian about her sexuality is exactly this: *Zip*. There is not a single baby book published today that doesn't have a lengthy chapter on love-making during and after pregnancy. But—and in 1990 I would say this is a rather large *but*—every one of these chapters addresses the love life of a husband and wife, primarily organized around the act of penis/vagina intercourse. Forget lesbians—there isn't even a footnote for single women, women with more than one partner, or women whose sexual habits fall somewhere outside the missionary position!

Let's talk about the question on everyone's lips: How did you get pregnant? This is not only the number one nosy inquiry of square straights, it's on the mind of every self-conscious lesbian.

You see, once again, the politically-correct thought police have established a pecking order for dyke conception. There is nothing so close to the macho fear, "Am I a real man?" as its matching Sapphic complex, "Am I lesbian enough?" The fact that gay girls get pregnant every which way short of immaculate visitation doesn't seem to have cracked the fear: Did I get pregnant the "right" way?

Most lesbians I know with children consider the matter of their conception to be a private matter, i.e., none of your damn business. Some say the discretion is to protect the child, but I say it's to protect the mother from insensitive heckling.

No one wants her sexual preferences called on the carpet because of the manner in which she conceived. Whether you do it with a straight man, a gay man, unknown or deeply loved, a turkey baster, a sperm bank, planned, unplanned, or predicated on the power of prayer, a woman's satisfaction at making a baby is not to be trifled with. Don't fuck with her.

Of course, lesbians have had babies long before the modern surge of artificial insemination. Taking the sperm into our own hands may be the emblem of the lesbian baby boom, but I think the boom itself is more a result of feminism and our economic independence. So many women are having babies on their own, with women spouses, men friends, and every other kind of newfangled family support. It's rewarding to talk about when you dispense with the stupid stereotypes.

Tell you what, I'll break the ice. My friend Hashima put it to me at a Christmas party: "Did you inseminate. . . or did you party?" I started laughing, and she winked. "Yeah, you partied."

That's right. I got pregnant the old fashioned way. I lay on a water bed with a real live man, someone whose genes and fatherly temperament I've been admiring for some time. Give me a love child. I'm pretty sure the TV was on, at least I hope it was, because all the cataclysmic sex acts in my life have been bathed in video incandescence. It was the first day of my ovulation and I remember visualizing the sperm being sucked into my cervix like a honey vacuum. It was thrilling. Biology as erotica.

The point of conception is an adventure no matter how you do it. My first science training came on the pump end of a turkey baster. In 1978, a group of five dykes tried to get our friend Beverly pregnant. Beverly lived in the country in a lesbian commune. She had a gay friend/donor who lived in a college town about ten miles away. We called him up one Sunday afternoon to see if he was in the mood to deliver a sample.

"Come over in fifteen minutes," he said. He produced the magic potion in a little glass Gerber jar which I cuddled inside my down jacket for the ride home. I knew it must be kept warm. There's also a time element, so I floored it and tried not to count the seconds.

Now for the fun part. Bev lay on a labyris patchwork quilt close to the wood stove. I flushed and cleaned the turkey baster a million times, worried that some previous vegetarian goo stuck inside would ruin our whole effort.

We were primed. Cheryl siphoned up the semen and entered the hard plastic tip in Bev's vagina. "Stick it up further!" we all said. Of course, everyone wanted to squeeze the bulb. And these were the days when possession of a dildo would have taken you on a neat ride out of town on a rail.

Well, we decided everyone could get one squeeze. A gang insemi-bang! We tried to "expect nothing" as we all knew Beverly was battling infertility mysteries.

We swabbed the outside of her os after fifteen minutes, smeared it on a little glass plate, and put it under our high-powered magnifier. What I saw through the lens that day is what I saw in my mind's eye the night I conceived.

"There they are! They're buzzing all around!" I said. I'm sure nothing this cool was ever performed in my high school biology lab.

Next: The Joys of 40D Breasts, Vibrating your Way Through Labor, and Should I Fist Fuck in the Third Trimester? Wish me luck—and send me your prenatal erotic fantasies, true life experiences, and more nosy questions!

Selected books from Cleis Press

SEXUAL POLITICS

Good Sex: Real Stories from Real People

by Julia Hutton.

ISBN: 0-939416-56-5 24.95 cloth;
ISBN: 0-939416-57-3 12.95 paper.

The Good Vibrations Guide to Sex: How to Have Safe, Fun Sex in the '90s

by Cathy Winks and Anne Semans.

ISBN: 0-939416-83-2 29.95;
ISBN: 0-939416-84-0 14.95 paper.

Madonnarama: Essays on Sex and Popular Culture

edited by Lisa Frank and Paul Smith.

ISBN: 0-939416-72-7 24.95 cloth;
ISBN: 0-939416-71-9 9.95 paper.

Public Sex: The Culture of Radical Sex

by Pat Califia.

ISBN: 0-939416-88-3 29.95 cloth;
ISBN: 0-939416-89-1 12.95 paper.

Sexwise

by Susie Bright.

ISBN: 1-57344-003-5 24.95 cloth;
ISBN: 1-57344-002-7 10.95 paper.

Sex Work: Writings by Women in the Sex Industry

edited by Frédérique Delacoste and Priscilla Alexander.

ISBN: 0-939416-10-7 24.95 cloth;
ISBN: 0-939416-11-5 16.95 paper.

Susie Bright's Sexual Reality: A Virtual Sex World Reader

by Susie Bright.

ISBN: 0-939416-58-1 24.95 cloth;
ISBN: 0-939416-59-X 9.95 paper.

Susie Sexpert's Lesbian Sex World

by Susie Bright.

ISBN: 0-939416-34-4 24.95 cloth;
ISBN: 0-939416-35-2 9.95 paper.

LESBIAN STUDIES

Boomer: Railroad Memoirs

by Linda Niemann.

ISBN: 0-939416-55-7 12.95 paper.

The Case of the Good-For-Nothing Girlfriend

by Mabel Maney.

ISBN: 0-939416-90-5 24.95 cloth;
ISBN: 0-939416-91-3 10.95 paper.

The Case of the Not-So-Nice Nurse

by Mabel Maney.

ISBN: 0-939416-75-1 24.95 cloth;
ISBN: 0-939416-76-X 9.95 paper.

Dagger: On Butch Women

edited by Roxxie, Lily Burana, Linnea Due.

ISBN: 0-939416-81-6 29.95 cloth;
ISBN: 0-939416-82-4 14.95 paper.

Daughters of Darkness: Lesbian Vampire Stories

edited by Pam Keesey.

ISBN: 0-939416-77-8 24.95 cloth;
ISBN: 0-939416-78-6 9.95 paper.

Different Daughters: A Book by Mothers of Lesbians

edited by Louise Rafkin.

ISBN: 0-939416-12-3 21.95 cloth;
ISBN: 0-939416-13-1 9.95 paper.

Different Mothers: Sons & Daughters of Lesbians Talk About Their Lives

edited by Louise Rafkin.

ISBN: 0-939416-40-9 24.95 cloth;
ISBN: 0-939416-41-7 9.95 paper.

Girlfriend Number One: Lesbian Life in the '90s

edited by Robin Stevens.

ISBN: 0-939416-79-4 29.95 cloth;
ISBN: 0-939416-8 12.95 paper.

Hothead Paisan: Homicidal Lesbian Terrorist

by Diane DiMassa.

ISBN: 0-939416-73-5 14.95 paper.

A Lesbian Love Advisor

by Celeste West.

ISBN: 0-939416-27-1 24.95 cloth;
ISBN: 0-939416-26-3 9.95 paper.

More Serious Pleasure: Lesbian Erotic Stories and Poetry

edited by the Sheba Collective.

ISBN: 0-939416-48-4 24.95 cloth;
ISBN: 0-939416-47-6 9.95 paper.

The Night Audrey's Vibrator Spoke: A Stonewall Riots Collection

by Andrea Natalie.

ISBN: 0-939416-64-6 8.95 paper.

Rubyfruit Mountain: A Stonewall Riots Collection

by Andrea Natalie.

ISBN: 0-939416-74-3 9.95 paper.

Serious Pleasure: Lesbian Erotic Stories and Poetry

edited by the Sheba Collective.

ISBN: 0-939416-46-8 24.95 cloth;
ISBN: 0-939416-45-X 9.95 paper.

FICTION

Another Love
by Erzsébet Galgóczi.
ISBN: 0-939416-52-2 24.95 cloth;
ISBN: 0-939416-51-4 8.95 paper.

Dirty Weekend:
A Novel of Revenge
by Helen Zahavi.
ISBN: 0-939416-85-9 10.95 paper.

A Forbidden Passion
by Cristina Peri Rossi.
ISBN: 0-939416-64-0 24.95 cloth;
ISBN: 0-939416-68-9 9.95 paper.

In the Garden of Dead Cars
by Sybil Claiborne.
ISBN: 0-939416-65-4 24.95 cloth;
ISBN: 0-939416-66-2 9.95 paper.

Night Train To Mother
by Ronit Lentin.
ISBN: 0-939416-29-8 24.95 cloth;
ISBN: 0-939416-28-X 9.95 paper.

Only Lawyers Dancing
by Jan McKemmish.
ISBN: 0-939416-70-0 24.95 cloth;
ISBN: 0-939416-69-7 9.95 paper.

The Wall
by Marlen Haushofer.
ISBN: 0-939416-53-0 24.95 cloth;
ISBN: 0-939416-54-9 paper.

We Came All The Way from Cuba So You Could Dress Like This?: Stories
by Achy Obejas.
ISBN: 0-939416-92-1 24.95 cloth;
ISBN: 0-939416-93-X 10.95 paper.

REFERENCE

Putting Out: The Essential Publishing Resource Guide For Lesbian and Gay Writers
by Edisol W. Dotson.
ISBN: 0-939416-86-7 29.95 cloth;
ISBN: 0-939416-87-5 12.95 paper.

POLITICS OF HEALTH

The Absence of the Dead Is Their Way of Appearing
by Mary Winfrey Trautmann.
ISBN: 0-939416-04-2 8.95 paper.

AIDS: The Women
edited by Ines Rieder and Patricia Ruppelt.
ISBN: 0-939416-20-4 24.95 cloth;
ISBN: 0-939416-21-2 9.95 paper

1 in 3: Women with Cancer Confront an Epidemic
edited by Judith Brady.
ISBN: 0-939416-50-6 24.95 cloth;
ISBN: 0-939416-49-2 10.95 paper.

Voices in the Night: Women Speaking About Incest
edited by Toni A.H. McNaron and Yarrow Morgan.
ISBN: 0-939416-02-6 9.95 paper.

With the Power of Each Breath: A Disabled Women's Anthology
edited by Susan Browne, Debra Connors and Nanci Stern.
ISBN: 0-939416-09-3 24.95 cloth;
ISBN: 0-939416-06-9 10.95 paper.

Since 1980, Cleis Press has published progressive books by women. We welcome your order and will ship your books as quickly as possible. Individual orders must be prepaid (U.S. dollars only). Please add 15% shipping. PA residents add 6% sales tax. Mail orders: Cleis Press, P.O. Box 8933, Pittsburgh PA 15221. MasterCard and Visa orders: include account number, exp. date, and signature. FAX your credit card order: (412) 937-1567. Or, phone us Mon-Fri, 9am–5pm EST: (412) 937-1555.